CW00802709

Farnell Teddy Bears

To my father

Dating from the 1920s, this 17-inch golden mohair Farnell teddy has already had some
restoration but his upper paw pads still need attention.

Farnell Teddy Bears

Kathy Martin

REMEMBER WHEN

First published in Great Britain in 2010 by
REMEMBER WHEN
an imprint of
Pen & Sword Books Ltd
47 Church Street
Barnsley
South Yorkshire
S70 2AS

Copyright © Kathy Martin, 2010

ISBN 978 1 84468 066 5

The right of Kathy Martin to be identified as author of this work has been
asserted by her in accordance with the Copyright, Designs and Patents Act 1988.

A CIP catalogue record for this book is
available from the British Library.

All rights reserved. No part of this book may be reproduced or transmitted
in any form or by any means, electronic or mechanical including photocopying,
recording or by any information storage and retrieval system, without
permission from the Publisher in writing.

Printed and bound in Thailand by
Kyodo Nation Printing Services

Pen & Sword Books Ltd incorporates the imprints of
Pen & Sword Aviation, Pen & Sword Maritime, Pen & Sword Military,
Wharncliffe Local History, Pen & Sword Select, Pen & Sword Military Classics,
Leo Cooper, Remember When, Seaforth Publishing and Frontline Publishing

For a complete list of Pen & Sword titles please contact
PEN & SWORD BOOKS LIMITED
47 Church Street, Barnsley, South Yorkshire, S70 2AS, England
E-mail: enquiries@pen-and-sword.co.uk
Website: www.pen-and-sword.co.uk

Contents

Childhood teddy bear of Miss Olive Mary Round MBE.

Foreword

When Kathy Martin asked me to write the foreword to this book I felt both honoured and – I'll admit it – more than a little apprehensive. It's my opinion, and one shared by many others, that Kathy is one of the world's top authorities on teddy bears. She was the editor of the much-missed *Teddy Bear Scene* magazine, has served as a consultant to stuffed animal manufacturers, and has written articles, essays and several excellent books about the world of artisan and collectable bears. Indeed, I've used her work to research some of the facts that have gone into the mystery novels that I write. So, what could a retired American police homicide detective turned mystery author possibly have to say about her latest volume dedicated to teddy bears, much less one focusing on the celebrated Farnell teddies? So, please allow me to present my *bona fides*.

My wife and I love teddy bears and have been collecting them for years. We spent our adult lives in the law enforcement service, working at a large police department in Southern California. It was a tough job and our teddy bear collection became a benign lodestone in a world that often seemed cruel and insane. Nowadays, we live in rural Virginia, where we're sometimes lucky enough to see real bears. Our house is full of teddy bears, but we've learned that there's always room for one more. If you're an arctophile, you know the sort of bear I'm talking about. It's the one that silently begs to go home with you and somehow looks happy when you're cradling it in your arms. Whether they're old or new, manufactured or created by an artisan, made from mohair or plush, teddy bears possess a powerful magic. They bring out a pure and childlike joy in people that's all too often missing these days.

Back in 2004 I wrote *The Mournful Teddy*, my first mystery novel set in the world of collectible, antique and artisan teddy bears. Mixing mohair and mayhem was an improbable concept, but I've learned to never underestimate the power of the teddy bear. The books became popular and sparked four sequels, each featuring some interesting bits of teddy bear history. For instance, in *The Crafty Teddy*, the plot featured the theft of a Farnell Alpha Bear. This allowed me to tell my American readers about both Farnell and how the Alpha Bear purchased by A A Milne eventually became the inspiration for Winnie the Pooh.

Which brings me full circle back to this wonderful book. As a retired homicide detective, I have to commend Kathy Martin's comprehensive investigation into the Farnell family, company and the bears it produced. Indeed, it makes me wonder if she didn't miss her true calling. As far as investigative ability is concerned, she'd have made a great cop. Furthermore, Kathy has achieved something both rare and incredible. She's conducted exhaustive research into all things Farnell and then converted the information into a superbly readable narrative. It's a first-rate history of not just teddy bears, but British culture during the first half of the twentieth century. The fact is, even if I cared nothing for teddy bears, I'd have devoured this book because it's a fascinating tale about a bygone time. Add the wealth of amazing photographs and you have a book that belongs on every arctophile's shelf.

So, turn the page and get ready to be entertained and enlightened as you read the true tale of the Farnell teddy bear.

John J Lamb
17 August 2009
Elkton, Virginia
USA

Teddy Bear Time Line

Key events of teddy bear history are listed in black; significant Farnell events are underlined.

1814
Joseph Kirby Farnell is born.
1860s
J K Farnell starts a business manufacturing fancy goods and toys.
1891
Joseph Kirby Farnell dies.
1902
German company Margarete Steiff GmbH creates first ever teddy bear (although the name 'teddy' is not yet used).
US President Theodore Roosevelt becomes associated with the new bear toy after refusing to shoot a captive bear during a hunting trip on the Louisiana/Mississippi border.
Shopkeepers Morris and Rose Michtom of Brooklyn, New York create their own stuffed toy bear following Roosevelt's well-publicised refusal to shoot the captive bear; demand skyrockets and Ideal Novelty and Toy Co is born.
1904
Roosevelt adopts the teddy bear as his mascot during his successful campaign for re-election.
1905
Steiff produce the first disc-jointed teddy bear (string and rods had previously been used); the disc method, which uses two card circles connected by a cotter pin, is still widely used today.
1906
Playthings, an American toy trade publication, coins the term 'teddy bear' for the

first time (as opposed to the previously used 'Teddy's bear', Teddy being Theodore Roosevelt).

Canadian-born writer Seymour Eaton publishes *The Roosevelt Bears: Their Travels and Adventures*, first in a wildly popular series of books about teddies.

Harrods advertises Steiff's 'soft jointed bear' in its catalogue.

1906–1908

J K Farnell produce the first British teddy bear.

1907

High demand sees the Steiff factory produce just under one million teddy bears.

1908

Dean's Rag Book Co makes a cut-out-and-sew printed cloth teddy.

1910

Harrods stock bears made by J K Farnell.

1914

Outbreak of the First World War sees UK ban on all German imports, including teddy bears.

1915

Other British toy firms including Chad Valley and Dean's Rag Book begin to manufacture mohair teddy bears.

1920

Mary Tourtel creates Rupert Bear for the *Daily Express*.

1921

J K Farnell & Co becomes a limited company; directors are Henry Kirby Farnell, Agnes Farnell, Albert E B Rose and Frederick Sully.

Daphne Milne, wife of playwright Alan Alexander Milne, buys a teddy from Harrods for first birthday of son, Christopher Robin; the bear is soon to be immortalised as Winnie the Pooh.

1924

Pooh makes a brief, unnamed appearance in *When We Were Very Young*, a volume of children's verse by A A Milne.

1925

Farnell registers its Alpha Toys trademark.

1926

A A Milne's *Winnie-the-Pooh* is published by Methuen & Co, with illustrations by E H Shepard.

Farnell exhibit at Leipzig trade fair for first time.

1927
Factory extension of 7,000 square feet is built at the Alpha Works.
Farnell introduces Anima Wheel Toy range.
1928
Farnell open City showroom in New Union Street, London EC2.
Agnes Farnell dies.
1929
Farnell advertise their new Silkalite Bears made from artificial silk plush.
Farnell open showrooms in New York and Paris.
1931
Farnell launch low-cost Unicorn Soft Toys brand and half a million soft toys are
    sold within first year.
1933
Lyricist Jimmy Kennedy writes words to the *Teddy Bears' Picnic*, the tune having
    been composed in 1907 by John Bratton.
Farnell introduce new teddy ranges – the 'Cheap Bear' and the 'Teddy Series'.
1934
Fire destroys the Alpha Works.
1935
Farnell open new, brick-built factory occupying 23,000 square feet.
The Alpha Bear is relaunched.
1937
Extension is added to Farnell factory premises to cope with extra business.
Farnell produce Mary Plain bears.
1938
Chad Valley receives Royal Warrant from Queen Elizabeth, wife of George VI and
    mother of Princess Elizabeth, later Queen Elizabeth II.
1939
Farnell chairman Albert E B Rose describes teddy bear as most popular soft toy
    extant.
The Second World War begins, temporarily halting virtually all production of
    British teddy bears.
1940
Farnell factory hit by incendiary bomb; three months later, the City showroom is
    also almost certainly destroyed.
1944
Henry Kirby Farnell dies.

1948
Screw-in safety eyes patented by Wendy Boston.

1953
Harry Corbett's Sooty makes TV debut and Chad Valley secure Sooty merchandising rights.

The Elms taken over by Middlesex County Council and turned into Acton Central School.

1955
First fully washable teddy bear demonstrated on TV by Wendy Boston Company.

1956
BBC cameraman Michael Bond buys a lonely teddy bear from Selfridges department store.

1958
Michael Bond's *A Bear Called Paddington* is published by William Collins.

1959
New safety eye with nylon screw introduced by Wendy Boston.

1960
Farnell open Olympia Works at 39 George Street, Hastings.

Farnell start producing Toffee bears.

Farnell introduce Mother Goose range of nylon-made soft toys.

1963
Olympia Works extended to 42 George Street, Hastings.

1964
All Farnell production ceases at Acton.

1966
Disney release *Winnie the Pooh and the Honey Tree*.

1968
Farnell's Coney Bear is displayed at London Design Centre.

1969
Publication of actor Peter Bull's *Bear With Me* awakes interest in collecting teddy bears.

1970
High Court orders winding up of Farnell; Olympia Works cease production.

1979
Marquis of Bath hosts teddy bear rally at Longleat, his country seat.

1981

Granada TV's adaptation of Evelyn Waugh's *Brideshead Revisited* brings fame to Delicatessen, an old bear belonging to Peter Bull, which is cast in the role of Aloysius.

1985

Opening by Ian Pout of Teddy Bears of Witney, the first shop in the UK to specialise in selling old and new teddy bears.

1988

Gyles Brandreth opens Stratford-upon-Avon Teddy Bear Museum.

1989

Alfonzo, a rare red Steiff bear which once belonged to Princess Xenia of Russia, is sold at Christie's for £12,100; bought by Ian Pout, he becomes figurehead of Teddy Bears of Witney.

Happy, a 1926 Steiff bear made from dual plush mohair, makes a world record at Sotheby's of £55,000.

1992

Steiff launch a worldwide collectors' club.

1993

Christie's South Kensington holds first auction dedicated to teddy bears.

1994

Teddy Girl, a 1904 cinnamon Steiff bear with impeccable provenance, sells at Christie's South Kensington for a new world record price of £110,000.

1995

J K Farnell & Co Ltd officially dissolved.

1998

Opening of Puppenhausmuseum in Basel, Switzerland, where visitors can see over 2,000 teddies dating mostly before 1950.

1999

'Campbell Bears' go on sale at Sotheby's.

2000

New world record for teddies set at a charity auction in Monaco when a modern Steiff bear dressed by Louis Vuitton sells for £130,000.

2002

Centenary of the teddy bear is marked by a flurry of commemorative bears and a special auction at Christie's South Kensington.

2007

Final teddy bear auction held at Christie's South Kensington.

1920s Alpha Farnell teddy bear.

Introduction

Although this book is concerned with the teddy bears created by the Farnell company, it tells a story that goes way beyond the confines of the nursery. Spanning a period of roughly 150 years, the previously untold account of the rise and fall of the house of Farnell begins in early nineteenth-century Leicestershire and concludes in a genteel English seaside resort in 1970. Along the way, the tale is punctuated by a cast of memorable characters and enough drama to satisfy the appetite of the most demanding soap opera devotee: driving ambition, business triumphs, business setbacks, imbecility, family rift, pregnancy out of wedlock, resourceful women, devastating fire and untimely death all feature in the story. In truth, the Farnell story is so fascinating that it is worth relating for its own sake, but what makes it even more compelling is the position of unparalleled importance J K Farnell & Co occupies in British toy history. For this is the story of the company that created Britain's very first teddy bear and then went on to produce the bear that would inspire a literary phenomenon, known to millions worldwide as Winnie the Pooh.

The importance of J K Farnell & Co Ltd has long been recognised by teddy bear enthusiasts – or arctophiles, as they are sometimes called – but surprisingly, until now relatively little has been known about the company's history. I first became interested in writing about Farnell when I realised that no more than the bare bones of the company's history has ever been published. My interest intensified when, intent on fleshing out those bare bones, I started doing some research and discovered that even the small amount of information that has been published is seriously compromised by inaccuracies. For example, one of the first discoveries I made was that the founder of the company was not John Kirby Farnell, as has been repeatedly stated in countless articles and reference books, but *Joseph* Kirby Farnell. It's a small point, to be sure, but it left me wondering how much I could count on the veracity of the bigger facts if such a basic detail as a name had been reported incorrectly. As I investigated some more I encountered further evidence of mistakes in the accepted version of the Farnell story. While part of me was excited to be uncovering a story that had never been told, I was also taken aback to realise that for years the true facts about this pioneering toy maker have been obscured. In its heyday, the company founded by Joseph Kirby Farnell was hailed by many as the world's leading soft toy company, yet today the name is known to few outside the rarefied world of the teddy bear enthusiast, and the true details of the Farnell story are known to virtually none. Therein lies my reason for writing this book.

Once I had resolved to write the history of Farnell teddy bears, I began the long process of unravelling the closely woven secrets of the past. Thanks largely to the existence of trade journals such as *Games and Toys*, learning about the company's products and its place in the soft toy hierarchy was not overwhelmingly difficult, but finding out about the people who ran the company proved much harder. In fact, I soon discovered that eliciting all but the most basic information about them was akin to searching for the proverbial needle in a haystack. Whenever I met anyone I thought might be able to throw a glimmer of light on the subject, I was invariably told that the Farnell family's involvement in the business had ceased during the Second World War. After that, nobody seemed to know exactly who ran the company – a few names were bandied about, but who they were and what their place was in the scheme of things was a mystery. Clearly, unearthing the truth was going to be more challenging than I had expected. It sometimes seemed as if the Farnell family had deliberately and expertly covered their tracks before disappearing from the teddy bear world. Ultimately, however, persistent research was rewarded by the revelation that, contrary to widespread opinion, Joseph Kirby Farnell's descendants were running the company that bore his name right to the very end. As with any history, some details remain unknown and some questions remain unanswered, but by and large I believe the facts regarding the origins, development and ultimate demise of J K Farnell & Co have now been uncovered. Through the course of my research I have developed a huge affection for the fascinating Farnell family so it gives me great pleasure to think that as a result of my investigations their story has been brought out of the shadows.

Exciting as these discoveries have been, however, the greatest pleasure in writing this book has been encountering the teddy bears, soft toys and dolls that made the company's name. The Alpha Bear, the Silkalite Bear, mascot toys, the Anima range and the Unicorn range – all these iconic products made a massive impact on the toy-buying public when they were launched. Trade literature from the 1920s and 1930s makes it clear that at the time Farnell was regarded as the premier British soft toy manufacturer and was 'unequalled in the world for quality and value'. Of course it was a British publication making these claims, but the success of Farnell toys both home and abroad proved there was some justification in the jingoistic pronouncements. Even today, among the cognoscenti the only teddy bears more highly revered than Farnell's are those made by the German company Steiff. Yet unlike Farnell, Steiff are still very much in operation today and have the benefit of a highly professional global sales and marketing team to keep their reputation polished and in the public eye. They also have the kudos of having invented the teddy bear, an achievement that wins them a lot of good will with the world's teddy bear enthusiasts. Considering these facts, the surprise is not that vintage Steiff bears generate massive excitement when they make saleroom appearances; rather, it is that without anyone around today to bang the drum for them and remind collectors of their exalted heritage, Farnell bears manage to achieve a close second to their German rival. By writing this book, I confess I am unashamedly picking up the flag once waved so enthusiastically in favour of Farnell by the staunchly pro-British *Games and Toys* journal. Not only was this a historically important and innovative toy manufacturer, it was also one that believed quality products and affordable prices were not incompatible with good wages and working conditions for staff. Oh, and it also created Winnie the Pooh. For these reasons, I believe the firm of J K Farnell & Co Ltd deserves a position of honour in the teddy bear hall of fame and a very special place in our hearts and minds.

An explanatory note about names

Like many nineteenth-century families, the Farnells had the slightly confusing habit of using the same Christian names for successive generations. For example, there was a John Farnell who was father to John and Joseph, and this first Joseph subsequently had two sons of his own named Joseph and John. As this second Joseph is one of the most prominent figures in the book, I have used both of his Christian names – Joseph Kirby – throughout in order to differentiate him from

A pretty Farnell teddy circa 1915.

his father who is referred to simply as Joseph. Similarly, when mentioning Joseph Kirby's brother, John, I have referred to him by both of his Christian names – John Wilson – in order to differentiate him from his uncle and grandfather. I have adopted the same practice whenever referring to a Farnell family member who shares the Christian name of a Farnell previously mentioned in the text, and also when the second Christian name is of interest because it illustrates yet another Farnell habit: that of using the mother's maiden name as a Christian name. (The term *Christian name* is used deliberately here since baptismal records exist for virtually all the key characters.)

Chapter 1

Life Before Teddy

So familiar and well loved is the teddy bear that it sometimes seems as if it has always been with us, bringing comfort and joy to children of all ages. Yet the truth is that compared with other traditional childhood favourites such as dolls, toy soldiers, balls, hoops and wooden arks, the teddy is a relative newcomer, having first appeared in the early years of the twentieth century. Even the teddy bear's forerunner, the soft toy animal, did not exist until the latter part of the nineteenth century and neither, for that matter, did the British toy industry itself, at least as we know it today. While other countries, notably Germany and France, were well known for their toy production, for various reasons Britain's toy producers kept a much lower profile, only emerging as a force to be reckoned with at roughly the same time that the soft toy was insinuating itself into the nation's nurseries.

In order to understand properly the role played by soft toys and teddies, it is necessary to look back to a time before they existed. Centuries ago, a 'toy' was not necessarily a children's plaything; instead, the word was understood to describe small, amusing or decorative objects that were created primarily for the enjoyment of adults, although by their very nature these objects would also have delighted any child that saw them. Popular 'toys' of this type were porcelain boxes, miniature figurines and dolls' houses, which were known at the time as 'baby' houses and were a great favourite with the aristocracy. Then, in the eighteenth century, the word became associated with the small silver items created by the Birmingham silver makers – snuff boxes, scent bottles, card cases, buckles, buttons and so on. These 'toys' were also intended for adults, but once again, because of their decorative nature, many were equally pleasing to children. Gradually, little by little, the word toy came to be applied to items specifically of interest to youngsters.

Of course it would be quite wrong to suggest that while the adults were busily admiring their finely painted porcelain boxes or arranging the furniture in their baby houses the children of the time were twiddling their thumbs for lack of anything to play with. They did have toys of their own, although for all but the richest these would have been homemade. Indeed, for the working classes, childhood as a concept did not really exist – babies were born and as soon as they were old enough to be useful they were put to work. For these children, playtime would have been an uncertain luxury, snatched whenever possible between working hours, and whatever toys they possessed would have been fashioned from rags, bits of wood and other odds and ends. This situation started to change towards the end of the eighteenth century when workers skilled in other specialised fields such as glass and watch making turned their attention to the children's toy market. Many of these new toy makers worked independently from home, buying the raw materials they needed out of the proceeds made from selling their last batch of toys. Their wares were necessarily cheap because they were bought by people like themselves with little disposable income. As a result, for most of these cottage industry toy makers it was a hand-to-mouth existence in which a period of low productivity would see the entire family go hungry. Even for workers employed by small toy manufacturing companies, conditions could be little better – wages were low and job security non-existent. Children were often employed making toys, particularly miniature or fiddly items, because their fingers were small and nimble and, of course, they were cheaper than adult workers.

Until the middle of the nineteenth century, toyshops were usually found only in the larger towns and cities. Even here, many toys were purchased from street vendors – often the wives or children of the men who made the toys – and in smaller towns and rural areas toys were sold by stationers, haberdashers and Post Offices, all of whom kept a few inexpensive but enticing items on their shelves in the hope of persuading a fond parent to part with a penny or two. In London, a popular location for toy buying was Lowther's Arcade, a glorious, glass-covered bazaar stretching from St Martin's church to the Strand. As early as 1859, the arcade was able to excite the writer George Augustus Sala, who described it as 'the toyshop of Europe'. He waxed lyrical about 'the honest, hearty, well-meaning toys of old England' while dismissing German toys as 'somewhat quaint, and somewhat eccentric' and French ones as fierce and warlike, 'smelling of Young

France, and glory, and blood'. Lowther's Arcade was famous in its day – literary luminaries such as Arthur Conan Doyle and J M Barrie (creators respectively of Sherlock Holmes and Peter Pan) mentioned it in their books and W S Gilbert of Gilbert and Sullivan fame co-wrote a pantomime, *Hush-a-Bye, Baby, on the Tree Top*, which was sub-titled *Harlequin Fortunia, King Frog of Frog Island, and the Magic Toys of Lowther Arcade*. From the contemporary accounts, it seems to have been a busy, bustling, magical place that sold everything from cheap and cheerful mass-produced items to the finest dolls and toys money could buy.

Things changed in the last decades of the nineteenth century with the rise of the department store. In these magnificent temples of commerce, toy manufacturers found a welcome new outlet for their products, although to begin with the stores did not have dedicated toy departments, preferring to sell toys seasonally. Thus, during the run up to Christmas they would be stocked with all the latest games, dolls and so on, but at other times they would offer little in the way of toys.

Sala's comments concerning the difference between English, German and French toys are interesting because they highlight the fact that, contrary to widely held belief, British toys were being manufactured at this time, even if a great many

The little elephant novelty made by Margarete Steiff for her sister-in-law, Anna.

were originating from cottage industry-type setups. It is often alleged that the British toy industry only became firmly established following the outbreak of hostilities in 1914 but Sala's glowing descriptions of English-made horses on wheels, 'bravely painted' millers' carts, carriers' carts, block-tin omnibuses, deal locomotives 'with woolly steam rushing from the funnels', brewer's drays, Noah's arks and many other items prove that toys of a certain type were being produced in Britain long before the start of the Great War. It is also widely documented elsewhere that a number of firms based in the Midlands made some wonderful tin plate items, notably Evans & Cartwright of Wolverhampton. However, the closest Sala comes to describing a soft toy is when he mentions 'noble fluffy donkeys, with real fur', laden with panniers and harnessed with soft brown leather. Although this may sound like the description of a cuddly toy donkey, in reality it would have been a floor-standing toy, more akin to a rocking horse (albeit without the rockers) than a soft toy. The truth is that before the 1870s the only commercially produced toys with any resemblance to soft toys were fur-covered animal automatons created by firms such as Roullet et Décamps of France. Thanks to their prevalence in European folk tales, bears were a popular subject for these wonderful mechanical toys, but they were almost always depicted as fierce rather than lovable, and in any case their delicate mechanisms rendered them unsuitable for hugging. These were toys to watch and wonder at, not to kiss and cuddle. It was to take, separately, an enterprising, disabled German woman and an ambitious Englishman with a large family to provide for to introduce the concept of a soft stuffed animal toy that existed purely for the pleasure of holding it.

A young German woman called Margarete Steiff is the person most commonly acknowledged as the originator of the commercially produced soft toy animal. Although she suffered partial paralysis having contracted polio in infancy, Margarete refused to let her disability define her life and, thanks to her flair with a sewing machine, she was able to found a toy-making company of global renown. Initially, Margarete worked as a dressmaker, but in 1879 she was inspired to adapt a magazine pattern for a fabric elephant cushion. Ignoring the printed instructions, she altered the pattern to create a little elephant made from felt. She called her creation 'Elefäntle' and gave it to her sister-in-law, Anna. Other female relatives admired the little elephant so Margarete gradually made some more. They were supposed to be pin cushions but to children's eyes they looked like delightful playthings. Margarete's lightbulb moment came when she realised the children were right: her elephants were toys in their own right. Encouraged by this positive reaction, she started to experiment and added felt dogs, cats, horses, rabbits and pigs to the original elephant design. The more she made, the more people wanted them, and thus her legendary toy company was born. By 1892 the company had produced its first catalogue, which featured the laudable maxim 'Only the best is good enough for our children.' Another step forwards came in 1897 when the Steiff company booked a stand for the first time at the Leipzig Toy Fair, the toy industry's most important trade event. Unable to attend in person, Margarete arranged for a new employee to represent her company at this prestigious fair. The young man in question, fresh out of college having just completed his studies at the Stuttgart School of Art, was to play a seminal role in the future of Steiff. A favourite nephew of Margarete, his name was Richard Steiff, and his gift to the world was the teddy bear, arguably the best-loved toy of all time, soft or otherwise.

Created in 1902, Steiff's jointed, soft stuffed toy bear, which did not become universally known as the teddy bear until 1908, made its debut in Britain no later than 1906 when it was featured in that year's Harrods catalogue. However, some toy historians believe Harrods had been selling Steiff's soft toys since 1895, although sadly the store cannot substantiate this due to a lack of departmental records, and no soft toys of any description are featured in their 1895 catalogue.

While there is absolutely no doubt that Margarete Steiff was an inspirational woman or that her nephew, Richard, was a massively talented and innovative designer, it must be acknowledged that credit for inventing the teddy bear has been claimed by others. The best-known rival claim cites America's Ideal Novelty and Toy Co as the originators of the teddy bear. In this account, a Brooklyn-based émigré couple called Morris and Rose Michtom made a jointed toy bear that they put in the window of their novelty store. It sold, further bears were made and sold, and ultimately a company – the Ideal Novelty and Toy Co – was born. Today the Michtom story is widely accepted as fact in the USA but elsewhere the majority of teddy bear enthusiasts believe the credit for making the first teddy bear, recognisable as we know it today, lies with Steiff, largely because the Steiff company has a great deal of supporting evidence in its archives. Weighing up the facts, it would seem that in one of those quirky coincidences with which history is littered, Steiff's jointed bear and the Michtom version appeared at roughly the same time, but the appearance of their bear toys was very different – although no

Model of Bär 55 PB standing in a reconstruction of Richard Steiff's workshop.

picture exists, the Michtom bear is said to have resembled a rag doll, whereas photos of Bär 55 PB, the very first Steiff teddy bear, clearly identify it as the forerunner of the classic teddy bear we all know and love. Thus, Steiff's claim to have given the world the teddy bear would seem to be firmly established.

Before the teddy bear, however, came the soft toy animal, and thanks to the Steiff company's excellent habit of carefully preserving paperwork relating to its history, there is documentary evidence to support the story of Margarete Steiff and her felt elephant. However, I think there is reason to believe that J K Farnell & Co may have been producing a type of soft toy prior to 1879, the year in which Margarete created her first elephant. Admittedly this evidence (which is given in full in Chapter 2) is not conclusive but it does at least raise the tantalising possibility that J K Farnell & Co created one of the world's first commercially produced soft toy animals. However, it is important to keep in mind that Farnell's earliest products may have been made from animal fur rather than the felt and mohair plush later favoured by the soft toy industry. Even so, since soft toys rapidly assumed a key place in British toy manufacturing – by 1924 the combined value of British-produced dolls and soft toys was higher than any other toy product, with mechanical metal toys coming a close second – the significance of Farnell as a trail-blazer is obvious. Interestingly, just as Steiff are believed to have supplied Harrods with soft toys from as early as 1895, at least one source suggests that Farnell were also supplying the store long before they made their first teddy bear. Writing in the magazine *Bear Collector* in 1997, Tony Ridgewell asserts that prior to 1910, when the company's teddy bears first appeared in the Harrods catalogue, J K Farnell was 'already a long established supplier of soft toy animals and dolls to the London store'. Sadly, as with Steiff, this assertion cannot be confirmed or refuted by Harrods, but when looking for a British manufacturer of the new jointed teddy bear it would have been logical for the store to choose a firm with which it had an established relationship. Furthermore, there is no doubt that Farnell maintained its prominent position in the face of stiff competition from rival British firms that jumped on the soft toy bandwagon in the early years of the twentieth century. *Games and Toys*, the leading trade journal for the British toy industry, made no bones about its opinion that Farnell was the market leader, regularly describing the firm as 'occupying a premier position in soft toy production' or variations on that theme.

The importance of the soft toy can be summarised thus: it paved the way for the invention of the teddy bear and was instrumental in developing a new industry that was to provide employment for thousands worldwide over the next few decades, and indeed still does so today. Farnell was a major player in the infancy of this significant industry, and although the company has not survived to the present day, its legacy certainly has.

Muddying the waters

An article that was published in *Games and Toys* in June 1954 could be the source of some of the most frequently repeated 'facts' concerning the Farnell company. This is regrettable since, although it is interesting, the article is flawed and it contains at least one extraordinary assertion that cannot help but cast doubt on the credibility of the whole. Written by Mr H E Bryant, at that time a director of Dean's Rag Book Co Ltd and Chairman of the British Toy Manufacturers Association, the article was published on the occasion of the fortieth 'birthday' of *Games and Toys*. Concerning Farnell, Mr Bryant's assertion that 'as far back as 1897, the late Mr J. K. Farnell was producing high class soft toys which were distributed the world over' is clearly false because by 1897 Joseph Kirby Farnell had already been dead for six years. This is nothing, however, in comparison with the astonishing statement Mr Bryant makes about the invention of the teddy bear. In his version of events, a (conveniently) un-named Englishman invented the concept of the teddy bear and then offered it to Margaret [sic] Steiff, who 'immediately saw the possibilities of such a production in England'. In short, Mr Bryant completely rewrites the history of the invention of the teddy bear. It is surely enough to have Richard Steiff and the Michtoms spinning in their graves.

Naming the teddy bear

The term 'teddy bear' comes from the nickname of US President Theodore Roosevelt. In November 1902, Roosevelt – known affectionately as Teddy to his friends and supporters – set off on a trip to help settle a border dispute between the states of Louisiana and Mississippi. As the president was known to be keen on hunting his hosts arranged a well-publicised bear hunt during his stay, but when the local bears made themselves inconveniently scarce it looked as if the excursion was going to fail in full view of the nation's press. The President was not best pleased and so in desperation the locals sought to rectify things by capturing an

President Theodore Roosevelt, after whom the teddy bear is named.

Did you know ...

that Roosevelt adopted the teddy bear as his official mascot when he was campaigning for the 1904 presidential election (which he subsequently won)? This, probably more than any other factor, helped establish the new toy in the public's affections and yet according to his great-nephew, Tweed Roosevelt, the great man nearly chose a completely different creature, the bull moose, to be his mascot. It is fascinating to contemplate what impact such a decision would have had on the teddy bear – would it have achieved such iconic status without Roosevelt's apparent endorsement?

old, infirm bear, which they tied to a tree. Roosevelt was then invited to shoot the pitiful creature but he declined to do so, declaring that he drew the line at such antics. (All the same the bear was killed, by knife rather than by gun.)

The President's refusal to shoot the bear attracted a huge amount of press attention and it was immortalised by Clifford K Berryman, a cartoonist from the *Washington Post*, who sketched the incident for his paper. The Berryman sketch was captioned 'Drawing the Line in Mississippi', a reference both to the boundary dispute that had brought Roosevelt to the area and to his decision not to shoot the bear. From the moment that Berryman's cartoon appeared in the *Washington Post*, Roosevelt had become irrevocably associated with the bear and almost within days his nickname, Teddy, was being used for the new jointed toy bears that were appearing in the shops. Initially they were referred to as 'Teddy's Bear' but gradually this was shortened to Teddy Bear. While the new name was widely adopted in the USA after the publication of the Berryman cartoon, it took somewhat longer for the Steiffs to accept it – they referred to Richard Steiff's jointed bear as Bärle until 1908, when they finally bowed to the inevitable and began calling it the teddy bear.

Chapter 2

Founding a Dynasty:
J K Farnell & Co, a Family Affair

Rural beginnings

Joseph Kirby Farnell founded his soft toy business in West London but his origins were a long way from the capital. The oldest son of Joseph and Eleanor Farnell, he was born in 1814 in Snarestone, a small village in rural Leicestershire. Kirby, his unusual second name, was derived from his mother's maiden name. Honouring the maternal side in this way seems to have been something of a Farnell tradition: Joseph Kirby's younger brother, John, was given Wilson, the maiden name of his grandmother, as a second name and both Joseph Kirby and John Wilson Farnell were to continue the tradition with their own children.

No precise details of Joseph Kirby's childhood are known but the relative prosperity of his family must have ensured it passed pleasantly enough. His paternal grandfather, John Farnell, was a well-to-do gentleman farmer with substantial land holdings and business interests in Snarestone and the surrounding area. The village of Snarestone lies approximately eight kilometres to the south of Ashby-de-la-Zouch, within a largely agricultural landscape. When Joseph Kirby was growing up it had a population of around 350 and the community was served by a church, a free school (where Joseph Kirby was probably educated), a public house and several skilled tradesmen including a blacksmith, wheelwright, butcher, boot maker and tailor. In such an environment the land-owning Farnells would have occupied a position of some importance and this would have been reflected in young Joseph Kirby's lifestyle.

In fact, Joseph Kirby would have been regarded by his contemporaries as a very fortunate child, because in addition to enjoying a comfortable start in life, he had a generous inheritance to look forward to, thanks to the unusual step taken by his grandfather of sharing his estate equally between his two sons. In the eighteenth and nineteenth centuries it was the custom for first-born sons to inherit the entire family fortune, thereby ensuring land holdings were not diminished, while younger sons had to make their own way in life. If they were lucky, some provision for their future might be made, but only if it could be done without unduly lessening the firstborn's inheritance. In this respect Joseph Kirby Farnell's father was far more fortunate than most since, although he was a second son, his father's will shared the estate equally between himself and his older brother, John. Additionally, Joseph was left a lump sum of £700 and a share in the family's woolstapling and hosiery interests. At the time, £700 was roughly worth £49,000 (according to www.moneysorter.co.uk, which uses figures supplied by the Office of National Statistics), a handsome amount for a young man to inherit. Although Joseph Farnell's father died in 1804, Joseph did not come into his inheritance until 1809 when he reached the age of twenty-one; until then his affairs were managed for him by his mother and older brother. Once he had reached his majority, however, he was free to act for himself and make his own decisions, one of which was to take a wife. In 1813 he duly married a young lady called Eleanor Kirby who came from Bicester in Oxfordshire.

Due to an absence of detailed historical records, it is impossible to know how Joseph Farnell came to meet, court and wed Eleanor Kirby, but bearing in mind that their homes were roughly seventy miles apart, a considerable distance in the days before the railway and the motor car, the likelihood is that they met through Joseph's involvement in the wool business. In addition to owning and farming land in Leicestershire, the Farnells were woolstaplers (dealers involved in the buying and selling of wool) and hosiers (merchants in woollen clothing) and under the terms of his father's will Joseph had received a lifetime interest in this trade. Eleanor Kirby's home town of Bicester had long been associated with the wool trade; in the thirteenth century it was granted a charter to sell wool at market and over the centuries the trade became so well established that one of the town's thoroughfares came to be known as Sheep Street. Moreover, Bicester is close to the town of Witney, famous since the seventeenth century for its woollen blankets. It seems quite likely, therefore, that Joseph encountered Eleanor whilst visiting Oxfordshire on business connected to the wool trade.

The couple's marriage took place in Bicester but they set up home in Snarestone where their first child, Joseph Kirby, was born in the spring of 1814. (Later in his life, Joseph Kirby would give his year of birth as 1816, but parish records show his baptism took place in April 1814. Strange as it seems to our modern sensibilities, before the registration of births became a legal requirement it was not unusual for even educated people to be a bit hazy about their birth dates.) Three years later the birth of a second son, John Wilson, would have been the cause of much rejoicing for Joseph, Eleanor and their extended family. Unfortunately their happiness was to be short lived because in 1822 – five years after the birth of John Wilson – Joseph Farnell died, aged just thirty-four. His premature death was probably a significant factor in the decision later made by his widow and children to leave Snarestone, but for the time being there would have been little outward change in circumstance for young Joseph Kirby and John

Joseph Kirby Farnell was baptised in April 1814 at St Bartholomew's Church, Snarestone, and his father, grandfather and uncle are buried in the churchyard.

Wilson. Despite the tragic death of their father, the boys would nonetheless have enjoyed a comfortable upbringing in Snarestone, with their uncle looking after their farming and business interests until they were old enough to do so for themselves.

From country boy to city draper

At some point, certainly no later than when they were in their twenties, Joseph Kirby and John Wilson Farnell decided to leave the familiar environs of Snarestone in order to seek their fortunes in London. The circumstances that prompted them to leave are something of a mystery since on the surface at least they had every reason to stay put. As the oldest son, Joseph Kirby would have inherited his father's land holdings and business interests, although if Joseph Farnell had followed the example set by his own father John Wilson would have received an equal share. Therefore, their leaving Snarestone is something of an enigma that can be answered only by surmise. One possibility is that their uncle bought them out in order to restore the Farnell estate to the condition it had been in prior to their grandfather's death. If Joseph Kirby and John Wilson had little liking for farming or found rural life generally irksome, then they might have been only too happy to sign away their inheritance in return for a large sum of money. Alternatively, it is possible that the Farnells' business interests had suffered such a reversal of fortune that the brothers' inheritance was greatly diminished in value. However, this seems unlikely since, as we shall see, Joseph Kirby and John Wilson had sufficient resources to set themselves up in trade in due course. The most likely explanation, therefore, seems to be that they sold their interest in the Snarestone farms and businesses to their uncle, John Farnell, thereby realising a sizeable sum of money with which to set up in an entirely different type of enterprise. It is worth mentioning that in swapping their rural home for urban living the young Farnell brothers were simply moving with the times: this was the heyday of the Industrial Revolution and thousands of people born to an agricultural way of life were migrating to the cities.

While the real reason Joseph Kirby and John Wilson Farnell left Snarestone may never be known, there is no doubt that they were living in London by 1841. According to the 1841 Census, both were working as drapers, but whether they were in business together or trading independently is unclear. Joseph Kirby's employment is given as 'linen draper' while his brother's is simply 'draper'. In the days before Britain's high streets were dominated by large department stores and retail chains, drapers – that is, dealers in cloth or clothing – played a vital role in their communities and were to be found in every town and sizeable village throughout the country. On arrival in London, the Farnell brothers would have realised that their wisest plan was to set themselves up in a business they understood and the experience they had gained from helping with their father's woolstapling and hosiery interests made the drapery trade an obvious choice. Since wool and woollen cloth was what he knew best, Joseph Kirby's decision to become a linen draper is harder to understand, but it is possible that he wanted to gain greater experience in order to broaden his horizons.

The personal circumstances of the brothers at this time are quite illuminating. Joseph Kirby was living in Pavement Row, Coleman Street, right in the noisy, bustling and exciting centre of the City of London. He was sharing premises with seven young men – all of whom are listed on the Census as linen drapers – as well as one male and one female servant. Although the information supplied on the 1841 Census is fairly limited (it does not, for example, identify the head of the household, as future Census returns were to do), the fact that Joseph Kirby's name is listed first and that all the other resident drapers are younger than him suggests he was head of the household and that the younger men were in his employ. Certainly his share of Joseph Farnell's estate would have enabled him to purchase an existing draper's shop or even start a new one from scratch. At the same time, John Wilson was living across the river in Lambeth, away from the commercial pulse of the city, sharing a terraced house with his mother, Eleanor Farnell, her unmarried older sister, Mary Kirby, and two female servants. Although Joseph Kirby and John Wilson were living apart, it does not automatically follow that their business interests were unconnected; the distance between Lambeth and Coleman Street was not so great that an averagely fit young man could not walk the round trip to work and back every day, or the business might even have been divided so that Joseph Kirby looked after affairs in the City and John Wilson headed up operations south of the river. Within just a few years, however, the brothers were definitely working independently of each other and on balance the likelihood is that this was already the case in 1841.

At this point it is clear that the real Farnell story differs greatly from the version of events accepted as gospel by most people. This oft-repeated and generally unchallenged account has a City of London silk merchant called *John* K Farnell establishing a business making pen-wipes, pin cushions and tea cosies in Notting Hill in 1840. With the exception of the surname and the City of London connection, every detail of the account thus far is flawed. In this inaccurate version of events (which is published in several books and on countless websites) there follows a period of fifty-seven years during which nothing much happens and then when the story resumes once again the facts are almost wholly incorrect. Fortunately, existing evidence makes it possible to know a lot of what really did take place during those seemingly empty years, with informed deduction filling in any gaps.

Starting a family

The most convincing reason for believing the Farnell brothers were working as drapers independently of one another in 1841 is the fact that Joseph Kirby had matrimony on his mind. In the nineteenth century marriage was almost invariably and fairly immediately followed by children so a man intent on taking a wife would

Interior of Docking Church, where Joseph Kirby Farnell married Elizabeth Burcham.

Docking Church

have to be prepared to accept the responsibilities of fatherhood. Without a welfare state to turn to in lean times, providing for his wife and family was a responsible man's overriding concern, and therefore Joseph Kirby, on the brink of matrimony, might not have wanted his business affairs complicated by a partnership with his brother. In any event, in the summer of 1841 he travelled to Docking in Norfolk to marry Elizabeth Anne Burcham. Although there is no record of how the young couple met, the occupation of the bride's brother does at least gives grounds for speculation. John Burcham was a Customs Officer at Heacham, a village situated about twelve miles from King's Lynn. Prior to her marriage to Joseph Kirby Farnell, Elizabeth had been living in Heacham with her brother, younger sister and widowed mother. Thanks to its proximity to the Low Countries, the Norfolk coast had long been associated with the import and export of wool and cloth, so it is reasonable to suppose that Joseph Kirby encountered Elizabeth Burcham and her family whilst visiting Norfolk on business. The village of Heacham has an interesting claim to fame – it was the birthplace of John Rolfe, an Englishman who travelled to the New World in the early seventeenth century and came home married to Pocahontas, the daughter of a Native American chief. A memorial to Pocahontas can be found in the church of St Mary at Heacham.

Like Pocahontas, Elizabeth said farewell to her family following her marriage, but unlike the legendary princess she was only required to travel the hundred miles or so from Heacham to London where the young couple began their married life, living in or near to Joseph Kirby's former Coleman Street address. They were still in London in 1845 when Elizabeth gave birth to a daughter, Eleanor Mary. She was their first surviving child, but given that the marriage took place in 1841 it is possible that there may have been one or even two previous babies that did not survive infancy. With the infant mortality rate hideously high at the time, few families escaped the trauma of losing a child. Indeed, records show that an Arthur Farnell was born in the City of London in 1843 and died very soon afterwards. While it is by no means certain, this boy may well have been the Farnell's first child; Arthur was certainly the name they gave to the son born after Eleanor Mary and it was a well-established practice in certain families to reuse the name of a deceased child.

Shortly after the birth of Eleanor Mary, Joseph Kirby moved his family from the filth and clamour of London to the relative calm of Shrewsbury in Shropshire.

Here he set up shop as a mercer and draper, occupying premises in Pride Hill, Shrewsbury's main shopping street. The move was probably prompted by a desire to escape the unhealthy conditions of the City. (Why Shrewsbury was chosen is unknown; the presence of several Farnell families in the general area at the time might have had some bearing on it, although there is no evidence that they were related to the Leicestershire Farnells.) During his sojourn in Pride Hill, Joseph Kirby's affairs clearly prospered: not only was he able to trade from a prestigious address, he was also in a position to employ an assistant, an apprentice and two live-in servants. A lodger – an accountant's clerk called John Case – brought in extra revenue that must have been welcome however well business was doing, because by 1851 the Farnell family had grown considerably. In 1847 little Eleanor Mary had been joined by Arthur, and Eliza arrived the following year. Charles Burcham was born two years after that and Edith in February 1851. It seems that after Edith's birth her parents had second thoughts about her name, and by the time the Census was taken a few months later she was being referred to as Agnes, the name by which she was to be known for the rest of her life. Elizabeth's hands would have been more than full caring for five small children, four of them under the age of five, so it is a relief to know that one of the live-in servants employed by Joseph Kirby was a nurse.

The precise nature of Joseph Kirby's occupation at this time is slightly ambiguous. When registering the birth of baby Edith (soon to be Agnes) in February 1851, he gave his occupation as draper. Just a few weeks later, when the Census of 1851 was taken, he was away from home, staying in Norfolk with his brother-in-law, John Burcham. Elizabeth, however, was at home in Pride Hill and she recorded her status as 'mercer's wife', further describing her husband's assistant as a 'mercer's assistant' and the apprentice as a 'mercer's apprentice'. Traditionally, a mercer was a textile dealer who specialised in silks, while, as has already been seen, a draper was a dealer in unspecified cloth and clothing. It is quite likely that the niceties of these definitions were not always fully appreciated by people and that therefore they may have been used interchangeably but, that said, it is inconceivable that a draper's wife would not have understood the distinctions. Additionally, given that providing false or misleading information to the Census was a punishable offence, it seems apparent that Joseph Kirby was indeed now trading as a mercer, probably as a complementary adjunct to his existing drapery business. In the status-obsessed nineteenth century, a mercer would have been regarded as a cut above a standard draper, so Joseph Kirby was on the up, and Elizabeth would have been understandably keen to broadcast her husband's improved status.

The fact that Joseph Kirby was in Norfolk when the 1851 Census was taken, staying at the home of his Customs Officer brother-in-law, indicates that he was still travelling the country on business. It also shows that this wife's connections were playing a significant role in the Farnells' lives and, as will be seen, they would continue to do so for many years. Whether Joseph Kirby saw much of his own brother during this time is difficult to say: having married a Wiltshire lass called Harriet Dawson, John Wilson had moved to Salisbury about a year before Joseph Kirby set up shop in Shrewsbury. He remained in Salisbury for at least fifteen years and appears to have prospered there. (Although John Wilson has no further place in the story of Farnell teddy bears, it is interesting to note that one of his children, Lewis Richard Farnell, became Rector of Exeter College, Oxford and Vice-Chancellor of Oxford University. He was an expert on Ancient Greece, a subject on which he published many books, and championed the unbiased study of religions.)

Return to London

Sometime between the summer of 1851 and 1854 Joseph Kirby said farewell to Shrewsbury and moved his family back to London, this time setting up home outside the City itself, in North Kensington. This area in west London was rapidly becoming popular with the newly affluent middle classes and Silchester Road, where the Farnells now moved, was a typical product of the property boom that saw smart semi-detached villas springing up close to more insalubrious housing. The homes in Silchester Road were connected to sewers, but just a few streets away desperately poor families were living in appalling, unhygienic slum conditions. Even in upwardly mobile Silchester Road, the more prosperous residents rubbed shoulders with poorer neighbours. In fact, there would have been no escaping the realities of poverty and deprivation, since the road was the location for a gargantuan steam laundry that employed women from the most deprived backgrounds. Required to work gruelling twelve-hour shifts, the women, who drank heavily to make their labour more bearable, would have been a familiar sight to the Farnells as they trudged to and from their work. For the children in particular, it must have seemed a very long way from the gentility of Pride Hill. No doubt Joseph Kirby and Elizabeth also had mixed feelings about their new circumstances, particularly as there is evidence to suggest that their fortunes had taken a temporary downturn. Even if, as is by no means certain, they were occupying one of the smarter Silchester Road houses, they were now living without the benefit of live-in servants, a luxury they had always been accustomed to – even when Joseph Kirby was single and living in Coleman Street, he was able to afford a live-in housekeeper. With two new babies to look after – Henry Kirby was born in 1854 and Martha in 1856 – Elizabeth especially would have missed the comforting presence of an experienced nursery maid. The arrival of Henry Kirby and Martha may well have sealed the fate of Eliza, the couple's second daughter, who was now packed off to Norfolk to live with her mother's family. Generally speaking, children were only farmed out to relatives when times were hard, in order to reduce a

Acton High Street as the Farnells would have known it.

High Street, Acton.

family's financial burden, although it should be noted that when the Farnells were enjoying undoubted prosperity Eliza remained in Norfolk.

Thus, when the Census was taken in 1861, the situation for the Farnells seems to have been less rosy than it had been ten years previously: the area they were living in was rather seedy, they were making do without live-in servants and one child was living a long way away, in the care of relatives. Perhaps most significantly, Joseph Kirby was no longer involved in the drapery trade that had kept his family solvent for over a decade. In Silchester Road, he was now an 'Agent for Servants' – in other words, he was running an employment agency finding domestic staff for affluent households. It was very different from his previous occupation as provincial mercer and draper and it poses the question, had he suffered some business misfortune or had he simply decided he wanted to try his hand at something new? With a family to consider, he would surely have been unlikely to risk embarking on a new career without good reason, so perhaps the Shrewsbury venture had turned sour after a promising start.

At this point it seems worthwhile to attempt a sketch of Joseph Kirby Farnell's character. From this far remove it is impossible to be certain but there is some evidence to suggest that he was a bit of a restless character. Having left his farming roots in order to make his way in the city, he abandoned that after a few years in order to try life in a provincial town. Then, just when his family would have started to enjoy a sense of stability, he uprooted them all and headed once more for the city. There may have been perfectly sound reasons for all these upheavals but on the surface they don't paint a picture of a particularly settled soul. He may not have been the easiest person to live with – restless souls seldom are – and the fact that his mother made her permanent home with his younger brother rather than him might support this supposition. However, the evidence also suggests that he was a man dedicated to providing a good standard of living for his family and his changes in location and occupation all seem to have been undertaken with the aim of improving his – and by extension their – fortunes. The move from Shrewsbury to Kensington may have been necessitated by business failure, but if so, Joseph Kirby did his best to house his family in an area that was at least 'on the up' and, as shall be seen, he soon found a way to augment his earnings as an agent for servants. So it could be that the underlying cause of his restlessness was a determination to succeed, to build a good life for himself and his family, and the perambulations from farmer to draper to mercer to agent for servants was simply a necessary process as he searched for the trade that would enable him to achieve his ultimate goal.

Change of direction and shifting fortunes

Luckily, placing servants in work was clearly something at which Joseph Kirby excelled. Within the space of ten to fifteen years he made enough money to relocate his family from the slightly seamy environs of Silchester Road to a more genteel home in suburban Acton. Just twenty or thirty years before the Farnells arrived there, Acton had still been very much a village rooted in the pastoral way of life. Wealthy families had country seats there that they visited from time to time but the permanent residents were country folk such as wheelwrights, blacksmiths, carters and so on. In other words, apart from its proximity to London, Acton had until quite recently been very much like Snarestone, Joseph Kirby's birthplace. All that changed when the railway arrived, giving city workers the opportunity to live outside London's grime and clamour. Suddenly a proliferation of new building brought streets of middle-class villas to the area, altering the landscape forever and changing Acton from pleasant country backwater to comfortable city suburb. Even so, when the Farnells arrived sometime between 1861 and 1871, the area was far less developed than it is today – it retained several farms and had plenty of green spaces between the new housing developments.

Joseph Kirby initially set up home in Grove Road, a short distance from Acton Station in one direction and Acton High Street in the other, with shops, school and church all within easy walking distance. He continued to work as an 'agent for servants' while at the same time developing a second line of business as a manufacturer of 'fancy goods'. The term was a Victorian catch-all for ornamental and decorative things that could not be otherwise classified. It was a term that covered a multitude of items – pearl buttons, lace trimmings and ribbons might be deemed fancy goods, as might sewing boxes and accessories, papier mâché trays, lithographed scraps, picture albums and innumerable other items that were indispensable to Victorian ladies. Drapers very often doubled as purveyors of fancy goods so Joseph Kirby was probably re-entering familiar territory when he launched into this line of business, but whereas he had previously sold the items, now he was manufacturing them. Quite how he made the leap from employment agent to fancy goods manufacturer is unclear but if he had a number of skilled workers on his books, looking for work as domestic servants because they could not find employment in their specialist field, it seems at least possible that he grabbed the opportunity to set some of them up manufacturing items for him. The 1871 Census reveals that he now had three assistants in his employ and these, presumably, were the people who made the fancy goods while his son Charles Burcham, now aged twenty-one and listed on the Census as a 'traveller' (as in commercial traveller, or sales representative in modern terminology), found stockists for goods.

A short digression

It is worth digressing here to consider the nature of the 'fancy goods' that Joseph Kirby was now manufacturing. It is an important point because if they were early examples of what we would today call soft toys, then perhaps Farnell had a head start on his famous German counterpart, Margarete Steiff, who is known to have created her first toy, a felt elephant, in 1879. While there is no firm contemporary evidence to prove Farnell was making soft toys in the 1860s and 1870s, there are references in toy trade journals of a later date that do support the idea. For example, in the February 1922 issue of *Games and Toys*, Messrs J K Farnell Ltd are referred to as having been established for over fifty years – in other words, since at least 1871. Nor could this have been a case of a reporter getting his facts wrong (as happened in 1968 when a snippet in *Games and Toys* erroneously declared that 'Farnells [sic] have been manufacturing toys since 1840') because in their advertisement in the same 1922 issue, Farnell themselves report that they have been 'Established over 50 years, for the best soft toys.' Furthermore, in January 1929 *Games and Toys* ran an extensive article about Farnell in which they stated that 'The firm has done much to demonstrate that the soft toy can be made a thing of beauty. It has led, and not been led, during the sixty odd years of its existence.' The quotation is doubly useful since not only does it signify that the year in which Joseph Kirby began manufacturing was no later than 1868, it also stresses Farnell's pre-eminence in the soft toy industry. This strong evidence would seem to suggest that sometime between 1863 and 1868 Joseph Kirby Farnell's company began manufacturing the sort of squashy, comforting, animal-inspired decorative item that would soon be known as a soft toy, perhaps becoming the first recorded business to do so.

There are those who say that the earliest toys produced by J K Farnell were made from animal skins – rabbit skin is sometimes specified. If this were true, it would mean that their soft toys were very different from the sort we know and love today. Since several teddy bear reference books repeat the animal skin story, most dealers and collectors have accepted it as fact. However, none of the books offer any corroborative evidence in support of the animal skin theory, and as no positively identified pre-twentieth-century Farnell toys are known to exist, I don't believe it should be taken at face value. In fact, it may well be that the word 'fur' has been responsible for some of the confusion. In 1891, Joseph Kirby recorded his occupation as 'toy and fancy goods manufacturer', making no mention of the materials from which his products were made. Nevertheless, two of his employees described themselves that same year as being employed in the 'fur toy industry'. Furthermore, a decade later Henry Kirby gave his occupation as 'fur toy manufacturer', although by 1911 all mention of fur had disappeared from these occupational descriptions. Yet as late as 1926, when mohair was indisputably the material of choice for Farnell's soft toys, the trade press was referring to the company's 'fur' products, suggesting that fur was sometimes used as a synonym for mohair. This conjecture is supported by the *Concise Oxford Dictionary*, which defines fur as 'the 'short fine soft hair of certain animals distinguished from the longer hair'. Compare this with the same dictionary's definition of mohair: (yarn or fabric from) hair of angora goat. Only when fur is used in its plural form – 'furs' – does the word imply animal skins with the hairs still on. Perhaps, therefore, the idea that early Farnell toys were made from animal skin arises from a misunderstanding.

Even if the Farnells did originally make their soft toys from animal skins, there is a possibility that other materials were also used. After all, with his many years of experience as a draper, Joseph Kirby would have had plenty of contacts in the textile industry and as an astute businessman he would have been ready to make use of any workable material that presented itself at an advantageous price. However, there are no existing records of the company's output from this time and without them it is impossible to be certain on this point. The situation is not helped by the fact that until the 1920s Farnell toys did not have permanent, sewn-in labels. Before then, flimsy paper labels were used, and because they were easily lost or destroyed few have survived, making identification of early Farnell animals extremely difficult. Add to that the highly perishable nature of toys made from animal skins and it is not surprising, albeit highly inconvenient for those interested in the history of soft toys, that very little is really known about Farnell's products prior to 1908.

Swings and roundabouts

Of course, back in 1871, Joseph Kirby had no way of knowing how significant his fledgling business would prove to be. As far as he was concerned he was simply working as hard as possible to improve his financial situation and though he was making progress there was still some way to go. Although she possibly had some daily help, Elizabeth was still making do without live-in servants, and whilst Acton was an improvement on Silchester Road, their neighbours in Grove Road were either upper-working-class types like the railway engine driver to one side of them, or lower-middle-class like the managing clerk on the other. Good, industrious people, to be sure, but not the social milieu into which Joseph Kirby had been born. Nevertheless, the seeds of his future success were sown whilst he was living in Grove Road and his mood must have been cautiously optimistic. Sadly, this mood would soon be broken in the most tragic circumstances when Arthur, Joseph Kirby and Elizabeth's oldest son, died at the age of just twenty-five. The cause of death is unknown, but whatever it was, the loss of their son would have been a grievous blow to the couple.

By 1878, the family was living a short distance from Grove Road, in the slightly more upmarket environs of Birkbeck Grove. Fate was now playing a game of swings and roundabouts with Joseph Kirby. On the positive side, his fancy goods business was doing so well that he was able to abandon the domestic agency in order to focus solely on manufacturing. It was also providing employment for his two surviving sons: Charles Burcham continued to work as a commercial traveller while young Henry Kirby worked as a 'fancy goods assistant', serving an apprenticeship that would stand him in good stead in later life. And now, at last, Joseph Kirby could once again afford to keep a live-in servant, a fact which would have pleased Elizabeth enormously had she still been in a condition to appreciate such things. That was where the 'roundabout' element came in, however: poor Elizabeth had now lost her mind, and although she was still living at home, she was officially classified as an imbecile. Indeed, it may well be that the servant, a very young girl who cannot have had much – if any – previous experience, had been employed expressly for the purpose of caring for Elizabeth.

This brutal classification of Elizabeth as an imbecile needs some examination.

Victorian attitudes to the mentally ill were generally less enlightened than they are today and there was certainly less understanding of the different types of mental illness. In the 1881 Census, there were just three categories in which the mentally ill could be classified – imbecile, idiot or lunatic. While lunatic was used to describe a person who was insane, possibly dangerously so, and idiot was applied to those born without any mental faculty, imbecile was the term used for people incapable of managing themselves or their affairs. It is impossible to know what brought Elizabeth to this sad condition but the death of her son Arthur may well have played a part, especially if he was, as has been suggested, her second son of the same name to die young. Thus, her 'imbecility' might in fact have been a nervous breakdown brought on by grief, or it may have been an age-related illness such as senility. In any case, the fact that she could be looked after at home rather than in an asylum suggests that her mental illness was not too severe or overly disruptive to the rest of the household. All the same, Joseph Kirby must have been struck by the bitter irony of his wife developing a mental illness just as he was on the brink of achieving the prosperity for which he had worked so hard.

Tragedy and turbulence

While business continued to prosper, as far as their personal lives were concerned the next few years were to test the Farnells' emotional resilience to the utmost. At the start of the 1880s, however, the future must have looked reasonably rosy, with Elizabeth's fragile mental condition the only apparent cause for concern. That was to change abruptly when a young man called Charles Monement came to lodge with the Farnells at Birkbeck Grove. There is a possibility that Charles was a distant cousin, on Elizabeth's side of the family. He was born in King's Lynn in Norfolk, the son of a doctor, and in 1871 he and his widowed father had been lodging in Heacham, Norfolk, with Elizabeth's mother and brother. While this does not prove there was a blood connection, it does at least suggest there might have been one, since the Burchams had already demonstrated their willingness to provide a home to needy relatives when they took in Eliza Farnell. As Eliza was still living with her uncle and grandmother in Heacham, she would have known Charles Monement well, but as she was twenty-one in 1871 and he was just fourteen she would not have considered him in a romantic light. That left the way clear for her youngest sibling, Martha, when Charles arrived at Birkbeck Grove a few years later. Whilst living in Acton he was pursuing a career as a commercial clerk and may well have been employed by Joseph Kirby in his toy making business. If that was the case, it did not deter him from making amorous advances to Martha. When she became pregnant, a marriage was hastily arranged; of course, Charles may always have intended to do the right thing by Martha, but sadly we have no way of knowing this. What is certain is that Martha and Charles Monement were married during the last quarter of 1882 and their daughter, Frances Marguerite, was born in the first quarter of 1883. Even supposing the marriage took place on 1 October 1882 and Frances was born on 31 March 1883, she would still have had to be three months premature for there to be no suggestion of impropriety between the young couple, and in those days there would have been no chance of survival for such a premature baby. The arrival of his first grandchild may well have softened any anger Joseph Kirby felt towards his son-in-law and the infant doubtless brought joy to the household, but sadly tragedy was once again lurking around the corner.

Within months of his daughter's birth, Charles Monement's mental health broke down (another indication, possibly, that he was related to Elizabeth Farnell), and he was admitted to Heigham Hall, a privately owned lunatic asylum in Norfolk, where he died on 20 June 1883, aged twenty-six. On his death certificate the cause of death is given as 'asthenia' following four weeks of 'prolonged maniacal excitement'. The term asthenia is not widely used today but it was once commonly used to describe weakness, lack of energy and loss of strength. Unless there was an underlying disease, it is hard to understand why Charles Monement should have died from such a condition so suddenly, and therefore the likelihood is that in addition to the problems with his mental health he was also suffering from a physical illness. Following her husband's death, Martha and her baby daughter continued living at 1 Birkbeck Grove while the rest of her family moved into the house next door. A new lodger was found, no doubt to help meet the expenses involved in running two households, but this time Joseph Kirby was careful to chose a sixty-eight-year-old widower who was unlikely to excite the passions of his unmarried daughters.

Pregnant, married and widowed within less than a year – poor Martha's life had been turned upside down by Charles Monement. Now it was the turn of her brother Charles Burcham to go through the emotional wringer. Having met and formed an attachment to a young woman called Edith Turner, the couple married in 1884, setting up home in Stoke Newington, an area some twenty miles from Acton. As shall be seen, there is reason to suppose that the marriage caused a rift between Charles Burcham and his family. In order to support his wife and the family that was soon to arrive, it appears that Charles Burcham started up his own toy manufacturing business, although no record of it exists today beyond his listing as 'Toy Manufacturer' in the 1891 census. In November 1885 Edith gave birth to a girl, Mary Eleanor, and in 1889 she produced another daughter, Beatrice Isobel. Tragically, the family had precious little time to enjoy the new arrival, because Edith died shortly after the birth of Beatrice. Now, unable to cope with his young daughters on his own, Charles Burcham sent them to live with his family in Acton where they would be well cared for by their Aunt Agnes. Despite the sad circumstances, the arrival of the two little girls must have been something of a godsend to Agnes, who had not married and, as she was now approaching forty, would have been resigned to the fact that she was unlikely to have children of her own. Furthermore, although her sister Martha and niece Frances were living next door, Agnes was now the only female residing at 2 Birkbeck Grove, so the presence of her brother's little girls would have been a welcome antidote to the overwhelmingly masculine tone of the household.

The arrival of Mary and Beatrice must have considerably lightened the gloomy atmosphere that inevitably followed the death of poor Elizabeth Farnell in 1887. Even though her mind had been disturbed for several years, her husband and children would have mourned her loss, especially Agnes, who seems to have been the daughter appointed to stay at home in order to see to the comfort of her menfolk. This was the lot that befell many unmarried women in Victorian times. Martha evaded it by marrying Charles Monement and producing a daughter while Eliza, sent as a child to live in Norfolk, for many years acted as housekeeper to her uncle, John Burcham, until ill health reunited her with her family in Acton before her untimely death in 1886. Meanwhile Eleanor, the oldest Farnell sister, took herself off to Brighton where she lived a seemingly independent life with just an eighteen-year-old called Edith Kemp for company. Edith's family was to have a long association with the Farnells – her parents lived in Acton, in a street about eight minutes' walk from Birkbeck Grove. Her father, Charles Kemp, was a music teacher, so although they were not well-to-do the Kemps were genteel enough for the Farnells to know them socially and, it seems, take them under their wing. In 1891, as well as giving employment to Edith as Eleanor's paid companion, the Farnells were also employing one of her younger sisters, Sybil, in their toy factory as a 'fur worker'.

Although Eleanor's move to Brighton smacks of independence it is likely that her house at 4 Paston Place was in fact purchased as a seaside retreat for the Farnells. With no income of her own, Eleanor would not have been able to run a separate household without help from her family, and as Paston Place is conveniently close to Brighton Pier and just a few steps from the seafront, the house would have made the perfect holiday location. Moreover, the Farnells had family connections living fairly close to Brighton. Henry Dawson Farnell, oldest son of Joseph Kirby's brother John Wilson, had trained as a doctor and was working as a general medical practitioner (GP) in Eastbourne, just twenty miles or so along the coast from Brighton. Living with him were his widowed mother and his siblings. Thanks to the excellent service run by the London, Brighton and South Coast Railway it would have been easy for Eleanor to travel the short distance to visit her relatives in Eastbourne whenever she wished. Later events would seem to confirm that the Farnells had a special liking for the south coast, and Henry Kirby was certainly visiting his sister in Brighton early in April 1891. It was also here that Joseph Kirby Farnell died in the December of that same year, at the age of seventy-seven.

Evidence that a rift existed between Charles Burcham and his father is found in Joseph Kirby's last will and testament. In the document, which is surprisingly brief for a man of business, he states that 'the business fixtures and stock in hand' are 'to be left and carried on by my three daughters and son, Henry Kirby Farnell'. Furthermore, Joseph Kirby bequeathed his 'furniture, household effects, books, linen, pictures and wearing apparel' to his three daughters, Eleanor, Agnes and Martha. Perhaps most surprisingly of all, considering the will was written at a time when women were generally considered unfit for business affairs, Eleanor and Agnes are named as his executors. While Henry Kirby may have smarted somewhat at the implied preference shown to his sisters, at least he was named in the will and received an equal share of the family business. By contrast, Charles Burcham's name does not appear anywhere in the will – nothing is left to him, not so much as a token, and throughout the will not even the most oblique reference is made to him. Even supposing Joseph Kirby had decided to exclude Charles Burcham from a share in the business because he was doing well enough on his own, he would surely have wanted to mention his son somewhere in the will, unless there had been a total breakdown in their relationship. It is impossible to know whether the feud continued after the death of Joseph Kirby but Census returns suggest Charles

Burcham did not move back in with his family, although his daughters remained with their uncle and aunts, and when their father died in 1918 he was living as a lodger in a boarding house in Norfolk.

By the standards of his time, Joseph Kirby Farnell lived a long and largely successful life – he certainly died knowing he had achieved his long-held ambition of providing financial stability for his family. More than this, he left them comfortably well off and with the wherewithal to build on his commercial achievements. However, the road to success had taken its toll, and despite their prosperity the Farnell family had been far from lucky. It may have saddened Joseph Kirby that of his seven children to survive to adulthood, only two had married, and

The Elms today, front elevation.

from those two marriages a meagre total of three grandchildren were produced, all of them girls. Of course, when Joseph Kirby died his youngest son, Henry Kirby, was only thirty-eight so there was still time for him to find himself a wife. Therefore Joseph Kirby may have been relatively sanguine about his chances of one day having grandsons to inherit his life's work, but even if he did feel this was unlikely, the preference shown to his daughters in his will suggests he might not have been too worried about male heirs. This would have been just as well because within two generations no one bearing the Farnell name would be running the toy company he founded, even though it would still be in the hands of his grandchildren.

It is tempting to think that the carved, collar-wearing animal that decorates the grand staircase in the entrance hall of The Elms might be a bear.

Upwardly mobile: the next generation

Throughout their lives, Henry Kirby and his sisters had lived in the shadow of their father's forceful personality. All that changed when Joseph Kirby died; for the first time they were able to make their own decisions, for better or worse. Fortunately, by this time Henry Kirby was well schooled in the toy industry – indeed, it was the only work he had ever known, having learned all about the toy trade at his father's side. As joint owners of the business, Eleanor, Agnes and Martha also had a say in how things were run, but it seems that they were conventional enough to want to let their brother take control, or at least to make it appear as if he did. Nevertheless, they would have made their opinions known to their brother and thus, by combining their talents, they were able to build on the solid foundations laid down by their father and go on to achieve even greater success.

The most obvious indication that the Farnells were making a roaring success of things is the relocation of the family in the final years of the nineteenth century from the middle-class environs of Birkbeck Grove to the grandeur of The Elms, an imposing, largely brick-built house located on the Uxbridge Road in Acton. The central part of the house, with a fine pediment supported by four huge Doric pillars, was built around 1735 and about twenty years later a new owner enlarged the property with the addition of an east and west wing. To complement this grand, spacious accommodation, The Elms boasted extensive grounds with greenhouses, a large fish pond and a boating house. Clearly this was a real step up for the family because only those with money could afford to live in a house like The Elms. Furthermore, by moving there the Farnells were making a very public statement about their status. Their great-grandfather had been a landed gentleman who would have been accepted as an equal by people living in houses similar to The Elms. Over the years his family had dropped a few rungs down the social ladder but now, by occupying The Elms – initially as a tenant and later as its owner – Henry Kirby was bringing them back to where, in his opinion, they belonged. Precisely when the move took place is unclear but thanks to an entry in that year's Kelly's Directory we know it was no later than 1898. Rather strangely, considering he had already been dead about seven years, the name of the householder is listed as Joseph Kirby Farnell. In fact, Henry Kirby was the official head of the household and the reason his father's name appeared in the directory was probably because The Elms now became the headquarters of the company named after him. Apart from its desirability as a gentleman's residence, the property had the advantage of providing sufficient space for a factory, which was built to the north east of the house. Thus the move there was sparked by a serendipitous combination of social aspiration and practical business consideration.

The family that moved into The Elms was a diverse assortment of widows, spinsters, bachelors and children. Living there with Henry Kirby in 1901 were his unmarried sister Agnes, now in her late forties, his widowed sister Martha Monement, her eighteen-year-old daughter Frances Monement, and his brother Charles Burcham's two daughters, Mary, fourteen, and Beatrice, twelve. Also living at the house, perhaps to provide him with some necessary male companionship, was John Scantlebury, the family's old lodger from Birkbeck Grove, plus four servants – a house maid, parlour maid, kitchen maid and cook – to help look after the household. For the Farnells, who had for many years

Although in a state of disrepair, the Farnell family grave in North Acton Cemetery is clearly marked.

managed without any servants, this quartet of live-in domestic servants would have been one of the surest signs of their improved social standing. By 1911, Eleanor had joined her siblings at The Elms, and she remained there until her death in April 1923. Agnes was the next to die, although she survived long enough to see married the nieces she had helped to raise. Martha died in 1941 and Henry Kirby lived on until 1944, reaching the age of ninety. He died in Acton, no doubt sorely missing his siblings but drawing comfort from his proximity to the toy factory that created his family's wealth. After his death, responsibility for J K Farnell & Co Ltd fell to his nieces, their husbands and children.

Chapter 3

Teddy Gets a Grip

(1908–1921)

I n the early years of the twentieth century people went teddy bear crazy. To begin with, it was the teddy bear's novelty value that made it such a rip-roaring success. There had been plush-covered bear toys before now but in appearance they had been quite unlike the teddy, usually positioned on all fours or else standing up on their hind legs in a vaguely threatening manner. The teddy bear, by contrast, focused on the elements that people found appealing in real bears – large shaggy bodies and comical, semi-human movement – and thanks to its jointing at the neck, arms and legs it looked more like a furry person than a real bear. Indeed, the use of the word 'arms' shows how completely divorced the teddy bear is from the reality of the natural world because real bears do not have arms at all, they have four legs. The dangerous aspects of real bears, such as sharp teeth, were completely disregarded or, as in the case of claws, translated into harmless stitches. (When a few adventurous manufacturers introduced teddy bears with teeth they met with little success.) The result was a revolutionary, non-threatening toy that appealed to girls because it was huggable and comforting and to boys for much the same reason, with the added benefit that because it was modelled on a bear it seemed more acceptably masculine than a conventional doll.

In retrospect it doesn't seem all that remarkable that children took to the teddy bear so quickly but what is surprising is the way in which adults also abandoned themselves to teddy bear mania. For a few years, it was all the rage for smart young people to be seen out and about with their teddy bears. Even though this trend faded after a while, it recurred from time to time – as late as the 1930s, toy manufacturers were producing bears in the fashionable colours of the season so they would match the clothes worn by their chic lady owners. There can be little doubt that the teddy bear's popularity with adults was driven by the proliferation of merchandise featuring its image that appeared in the early years of the twentieth century. Teddy bears appeared everywhere: in books and advertisements, on postcards and porcelain products; even mundane household goods made use of the teddy bear's cosy image.

It did not take long for other toy manufacturers to jump on the teddy bear bandwagon. In Germany, Steiff soon had competition from Gebrüder Bing, Crämer, Strunz and various others, while in the US Ideal had many rivals, although they appear to have come and gone with remarkable rapidity. In Britain, however, the toy manufacturers' response to the teddy bear phenomenon was initially more cautious; despite all the hype, the prevailing opinion seems to have been that the new toy might be a flash in the pan. Without a home-produced bear to satisfy demand, the only option was to import them, and thus Steiff teddy bears became the first to be sold in Britain. The first consignment of Steiff bears is believed to have reached England in 1905 and, thanks to their appearance in the Harrods catalogue of 1906, it is a known fact that the store was selling them by then. Alas, there is less certainty about when the first British-made teddy bear was produced, since 1906, 1908 and 1910 have all been put forward as likely years. However, whenever the first British teddy bear did appear, most experts agree that it was created by J K Farnell & Co.

1906, 1908 or 1910?

As the year of initial production and the identity of the first manufacturer are important historical details, it is worth spending some time examining the various claims and their supporting evidence. The earliest date is put forward by former Christie's teddy bear specialist Leyla Maniera in her 2001 book *Christie's Century of Teddy Bears*. In a section dealing with the birth of the British bear, she states that teddies featured in the 1906 catalogues of J K Farnell. This is a very exciting claim which, if supported by an image of the catalogue in question, would prove the point conclusively. Regrettably, however, no such image is shown in the book and it has not been possible to ascertain from the author whether she herself has seen a copy of the 1906 catalogue or simply learned of its existence from another source. It is most unlikely that a respected and knowledgeable teddy bear professional like Leyla Maniera would have made the claim without being sure of her facts, but all the same, physical evidence would have removed any lingering

TY 365. English Made Model Plush Teddy Bears of fine quality, complete with growl. 11½ in. 4/6, 13 in. 6/6, 14½ in. 8/6, 16 in. 10/6, 18 in. 13/6, 20 in. 17/6, 22 in. 21/0, 24 in. 25/6, 26 in. 31/6

HARRODS Limited, Brompton Road, London, S.W.

TOY DEPARTMENT.
TEDDY BEARS, ETC.

T.Y. 147. £5-5-0
TY 767 7/6
TY 768 £6-6-0
TY 755 (11 2/11 3/11)
TY 762 35/6
TY 744 10/6
TY 742 3/6

TY 365
4/6
6/6
8/6
10/6
13/6
21/-
25/6
27/6
31/6

T.Y. 142. Mr. Golliwogg, fine knockabout toy, 20 in. high. 3 6
T.Y. 755. Jemima Puddle Duck, life-like model. Size 8 in., 1 11; 10 in., 2 11; 13 in., 3 11
T.Y. 757. Model Skye Terrier, fine plush, 8 in. high x 11 in. long 7 11
T.Y. 760. Model Chocolate Pom, fine coat, 11½ in. high, 15 in. long 12 6
T.Y. 758. Model Lamb, with voice, on wheels, 15 in. high, 14 in. long, 14 11
T.Y. 756. Model Terrier, fine quality plush, 9 in. high 3 11
T.Y. 759. Lucky Black Cat, with squeak, fine plush, 11 in. high ... 2 11
T.Y. 744. Model Skin Horse on wheels, with harness complete, 13 in. high, 10 6
T.Y. 748. Model Plush Bear on wheels, with squeak, 26 in. high, 28 in. long £2 12 6
T.Y. 768. Model Plush Buffalo on wheels, 33 in. high, 39 in. long ... 6 Gns.
T.Y. 762. Model Felt Donkey on wheels, 26 in. high, 30 in. long 35 6
T.Y. 365. Growing Teddy Bears, life-like models, superior plush, 11½ in., 4 6; 13 in., 6 6; 14½ in., 8 6; 16 in., 10 6; 18 in., 13 6; 20 in., 21 0; 22 in., 25 6; 24 in., 27 6; 26 in., 31 6
T.Y. 765. White Muff Teddy Bear, with squeak, fine quality plush, 28 in. long, 8 in. wide, 7 11
T.Y. 767. Coloured Plush Balls, soft or solid 1 6
T.Y. 770. Animated Model "King Charles" Spaniel. Size 10 in. 2 11
T.Y. 751. Model Plush Water Spaniel, with squeak, 9 in. high, 14 in. long ... 7 11
T.Y. 749. Model Plush Rabbit, grey and white, with voice, 17 in. long ... 9 6
T.Y. 750. The Famous "Cæsar" Dog, complete with collar, 7 in. high, 10½ in. long, 2 6
T.Y. 751. Harrods Lucky Black Cat Family, 11 in., 6 in., 4 in. high. ... Complete 3 6
T.Y. 745. Velvet Cosy Lucky Black Cat, 11 in. high, 12 in. wide ... 3 9
T.Y. 764. Shackleton's Model Plush Penguins, with squeak, 9 in., 1 11; 11 in., 2 11; 13 in., 4 6; 15 in., 5 11
T.Y. 766. Harrods Esquimaux Family, Pa, Ma, and the Mites. Pa and Ma, 15 in., the Mites, 9 in. Set complete, 21 0
T.Y. 752. Model Plush Irish Terrier, complete with collar. Size 13 in. 8 6
T.Y. 753. Model Plush Irish Terrier on wheels, 13 in. high, 13 in. long, 7 11
T.Y. 754. Model Brown Plush Spaniel, with squeak, 9½ in. high, 17 in. long, 15 11
T.Y. 747. Travelling Rocking Horse, skin covered. Mechanical action. Height to saddle, 28 in.; length of stand, 32 × 14 in., 5 Gns.
T.Y. 746. Plush Chimpanzee, splendid model, 23 in. long, 25 6
T.Y. 769. Model Skin Bulldog on wheels, 18½ in. high, 20 in. long 55 6
T.Y. 743. Model Soft Bear on wheels, 19 in. high, 25 in. long, 45 6

TY 751 7/11
TY 751 55/6
TY 764 15/11
TY 764 1/11 2/11 4/6 5/11
TY 760 12/6
TY 757 7/11
TY 761 3/6
TY 759 14/11

Top left: The webbed claw stitching visible in Harrods' 1912 catalogue helps identify TY 365 as a Farnell.

Above: Page from 1910 Harrods catalogue showing TY 365.

Left: TY 365 appeared in the Harrods Christmas catalogue of 1910.

doubt on the subject. Strenuous attempts to trace the catalogue have proved fruitless but this is not overly surprising since surviving Farnell catalogues from any year are few and far between.

In the absence of conclusive evidence in support of the 1906 claim, the alternative candidate years cannot be disregarded out of hand. Those favouring 1908 as the year the British teddy bear made its debut maintain that this was when Joseph Eisenmann, a German-born, British-naturalised toy dealer who imported Steiff bears into Britain, persuaded Farnell to start producing their own version because demand was outstripping supply. It is a highly plausible story – Eisenmann had been living in London since around 1881 and had become well connected through his work in the toy trade. All the same, in order to raise the status of the story from hearsay to fact, some hard evidence is needed. On the other hand, while evidence proving that British teddy bears were being manufactured by 1910 does exist (see below), it does not necessarily follow that this was the first year in which they were produced. In fact, as the evidence comes in the form of illustrations in two separate Harrods catalogues published in 1910 – a general catalogue and a later special Christmas edition – it seems likely that the bears would have been made sometime during the previous year, and possibly even before that. After all, the first Steiff bears reportedly arrived in Britain in 1905, but did not make their debut in the Harrods catalogue until the following year. Therefore, it is probably safe to eliminate 1910 from contention, but that still leaves 1906 and 1908 in the running for that all-important year. The truth is that until some further solid evidence comes to light – such as a copy of the 1906 Farnell catalogue – we'll never be entirely sure of exactly when the British toy manufacturers dipped a first tentative toe into the teddy bear market.

Farnell and Harrods

Amidst all this uncertainty, it is good to have some facts that are undisputed. It is thanks to Harrods and their catalogues that we can be absolutely sure that British teddy bears were being produced no later than 1910. In their main catalogue of that year, a photographic image of a teddy bear appears on a page advertising a number of different soft toys. The teddy is identified as TY 365 and the description reads as follows: 'Teddy Bears, Superior Plush and Life-like Models, with Growl, 4/6, 6/6, 8/6, 10/6, 13/6, 17/6, 21/0, 25/6, 31/6.'

A different image of the same teddy appears in the 1910 Christmas edition of

A small Farnell teddy bear dating from 1910–1915.

the catalogue, with the wording altered slightly: 'Growling Teddy Bears, life-like models, superior plush, 11 $^1/_2$ in., **4/6**; 13 in., **6/6**; 14 $^1/_2$ in., **8/6**; 16 in., **10/6**; 18 in., **13/6**; 20 in., **21/0**; 22 in., **25/6**; 24 in., **27/6**; 26 in., **31/6**.'

Although the teddy's country of origin is not identified in either of the two 1910 catalogues, an illustration of the same bear – TY 365 – is featured in the 1912 catalogue and this time the wording clearly states that it is English made. The crucial evidence here is the reference number TY 365, which identifies the English-made bear in the 1912 catalogue as the same one featured in the catalogues of 1910, and the point is reinforced by the fact that the size options and prices are identical in all three catalogues.

The next big question concerns the identity of the 'English-made' bear's manufacturer and there are three compelling pieces of evidence that point in the direction of Farnell. Harrods at this time were not in the habit of identifying their suppliers but close scrutiny of the image in their 1910 Christmas catalogue reveals a vital clue in the shape of webbed claw stitching on the teddy's paw. Four teddy

During the First World War the ban on German imports encouraged manufacturers such as W H Jones to start competing with Farnell in the teddy bear market.

AN INVITATION TO VISIT
OUR SHOWROOMS

Buyers coming to London should make an early inspection of our special range of

SOFT TOYS
FOR 1915

MANUFACTURED IN LONDON.

Teddy Bears, Esquimaux Dolls, DOLLS, DOGS, RABBITS, etc., and **MILITARY SETS.**

Wholesale and Export Only.

Manufacturer :—

W. H. JONES,

49, Red Cross St., London, E.C.   'Phone :— City 7421.

bear manufacturers – J K Farnell, W J Terry, Eisenmann & Co (often known as Einco) and Merrythought – are known to have used webbed claw stitching, but W J Terry did not produce teddies until around 1913, Eisenmann & Co a couple of years later and Merrythought did not come into existence until 1930. Furthermore, each manufacturer had its own way of stitching the webbed claws and while they may look identical at first glance, closer study reveals subtle differences. By using a magnifying glass to look at the photograph of TY 365 in the 1910 Harrods Christmas catalogue, it can be seen that the claw stitching matches that found on early Farnell teddy bears. Then there is the overall appearance of TY 365, which closely resembles Farnell bears known to date from this period. Finally, Farnell themselves maintained they were Britain's teddy bear pioneers and none of their rivals disputed the claim, which they most surely would have done had there been any question on the point. Taken together, there seems no doubt that Farnell was the manufacturer of TY 365, the first teddy bear to be positively identified as British made.

An industry nurtured by war

Having started the ball rolling with British teddy bear production, the people at Farnell soon discovered they were not going to have this lucrative new market entirely to themselves. Within just a year or so, another London-based firm, the British United Toy Manufacturing Co Ltd, began producing teddy bears. They used the trade name 'Omega' and, perhaps because the full name is such a mouthful, this is the name collectors generally use when referring to the company's products. Very soon, William J Terry, a Hackney-based toy maker, was also manufacturing teddies and, as has been noted, these toys bore strong similarities to Farnell's output. (Interestingly, before Terry moved to Hackney, the company had occupied premises in Stoke Newington; this was around the same time that Charles Burcham Farnell was living in Stoke Newington, working – according to his 1891 Census listing – as a 'toymaker'. Was Charles Burcham working for Terry, a rival of his family's soft toy company, and if so, was this the cause of the rift or simply a result of it?) While these rivals scarcely presented Farnell with an avalanche of home-grown competition, it is possible that other British companies, whose names and products are not remembered today, were also making teddy bears at this time. In any case, everything was soon to change with the advent of the First World War.

In Sarajevo on 28 June 1914, a Bosnian-Serb student called Gavrilo Princip assassinated Archduke Franz Ferdinand, the heir to the Austro-Hungarian Empire, and in so doing set in train a chain of events that would lead to worldwide conflict on an unprecedented scale. Tension had been brewing in Europe for years as the leading powers formed alliances and flexed their military muscles by building up their army and navy capabilities. Princip's action provided the spark that made this tension erupt. When the Austrians, convinced that the Serbs were complicit in the assassination of Franz Ferdinand, declared war against Serbia, existing alliances led Russia, France and Britain to pitch in on the side of the Serbs while Germany duly sided with Austria. By early August the major European nations were at war and because most of them had colonies outside Europe, the conflict spread worldwide. The prevailing opinion was that the war would be over by Christmas but in fact it dragged on until November 1918 and cost an estimated sixteen million lives. It came to be called the Great War because of the scale on which it was fought and the number of casualties it caused.

While the war brought hardship and misery to untold millions, it played a pivotal role in the development of a significant British teddy bear industry. At the outset of the war, a ban on German imports and a backlash of opinion against anything perceived to have come from 'the enemy' left toy retailers with a problem, since the teddy bear was still very much in demand. Intense patriotic fervour abounded, so much so that shops attempting to sell existing stock of German-made products were harshly criticised. Added to this, reciprocal bans imposed by Germany on British goods meant the English mohair trade lost its lucrative German markets. With a public demanding teddy bears and a ready supply of the material needed to make them, the British toy manufacturers were finally galvanised into action and by 1915 were producing high-quality bears of their own. Farnell now faced new competition from established toy companies like Chad Valley, Chiltern (a trade name of Eisenmann & Co) and Dean's Ragbook Company Ltd as well as from newcomers such as W H Jones and Harwin & Co, a firm founded in 1914, which became famous for its bears dressed in the uniforms of Britain and her allies.

This new surge of teddy bear production might have alarmed Farnell but thanks to the company's pre-eminence in the soft toy field they were able to withstand the onslaught, maintaining their presence with Harrods as evidenced by the

This extremely rare pin-jointed Farnell was produced during the First World War when German imports were banned.

Tiny Farnell bears were given as good luck mascots to soldiers headed to the Front.

appearance of TY 365 in the store's 1916 gift catalogue. Even so, Farnell realised this was no time for a company to rest on its laurels. Aware of the need to react to a changing market, they introduced a new line in bears: a fully jointed miniature mohair teddy bear that was exactly the right size to pop in a serviceman's pocket as a good luck mascot. The bears had rather comical upturned faces that were designed to peep out of a uniform pocket. Known to collectors today as 'Soldier Bears' (a term coined by a well-known dealer in vintage teddy bears), these little teds were produced by Farnell in the customary golden mohair as well as in the highly patriotic colours of red, white and blue. When they occasionally crop up at auction they tend to attract a lot of attention, none more so than the astonishing collection known as the Campbell Bears, which was sold by Sotheby's in May 1999 (see Chapter 8). As well as the tiny teddies, Farnell also made mascot cats and dogs, one of which may have accompanied A A Milne to the Somme. In her 1990 biography of Milne, Ann Thwaite reveals how the writer's wife, Daphne, slipped the mascot dog into her husband's bag on his last morning in England. According to Daphne Milne, her husband used to claim that Carmen, the toy dog, saved him from the Somme by catching and passing on to him the germ that causes trench fever. If the little dog was made by Farnell – and there is a strong possibility that it was – then it was the precursor of that other Farnell toy whose association with the Milne family would turn it into a household name and a global phenomenon.

Jobs for the girls

While some British teddy bear manufacturers undoubtedly owed their growth to the absence of German competition during the war years (1914–1918), this was not the case with J K Farnell & Co, who were already doing extremely well before hostilities broke out. According to information given to a Board of Trade Committee just after the end of the war, in 1913 the firm employed 189 factory workers and 50 outworkers. These statistics put paid to the belief harboured by many that even in its heyday Farnell was not much more than a cottage industry. On the contrary, as a significant local employer, the company would have been much appreciated within the Acton community for bringing job security to many – mostly teenage girls and women, as the majority of workers in the soft toy industry were female. In Farnell's case, this predominance of women was carried through to the highest level of the company, since three of the four joint owners were female. Under the terms of Joseph Kirby Farnell's will, his three surviving daughters – Eleanor and Agnes Farnell and Martha Monement – were equal partners with their brother, Henry Kirby Farnell. It is unclear how closely involved the sisters were in the day-to-day running of the company but clues found in the will of Agnes Farnell suggest that she was very familiar with some of the employees and such familiarity could only have come from meeting them on the factory floor.

As joint owners of a flourishing business, the Farnell sisters were unusual in pre-First World War society. They owed their status to their father's affection and probably also to his awareness of their abilities, but at the time not many women were as fortunate. Although changes were afoot, women still did not have the right to vote and were regarded by many diehard misogynists as an abhorrence in the workplace. While it was acceptable for a girl to work as a servant, nurse, teacher, shop assistant or waitress, most other occupations were frowned upon. However, the soft toy industry appears to have been one of the few employment arenas in which women could rise to positions of authority, even before the shortage of men caused by the war made this more commonplace. As was so often the case, Farnell was at the forefront of change, having appointed a woman to the role of factory manager by 1911. The woman in question, Sybil Kemp, was thirty-six years old in 1911 and she had worked for J K Farnell & Co since she was at least fifteen. Her father was a professor of music, a reasonably genteel occupation, but one that did not bring in enough income for him to let his three daughters live as ladies of leisure. As we have seen, the eldest girl, Edith, worked as a paid companion to Eleanor Farnell in Brighton before returning to London to become a stationer's assistant. The youngest daughter, Ethel, followed Edith into shop work when she was employed by a confectioner although she later became a bookkeeper. However, the middle daughter, Sybil, began her working life as a 'fur worker' with J K Farnell & Co and rose to the important position of factory manager, responsible for the productivity of over 150 workers. She has also been credited with designing many of Farnell's products and while proof of this has been hard to come by it would seem quite likely that she did – after all, having worked for the company for many years she would have had a solid grasp of how the toys were made and as a bright young woman would doubtless have had many ideas of her own.

Another woman who seems to have played a fairly important role in the Farnell hierarchy at this time was Alice Upstone. Alice and her older sister Emma worked for Farnell in the 1890s in an unspecified capacity, the 1891 Census recording simply that they assisted in the toy business. By 1911, however, Alice was employed by the company as a clerk – a job title that was more highly respected than it is today – and she was evidently regarded by Agnes Farnell with trust and affection, as shall be seen in the following chapter. (Alice's sister Emma had left Farnell and was now keeping house for her sister and her brother, a railway clerk.) The names of two other female employees from this era are known. Minnie and Jessie Prowse were daughters of Ealing coachman George Prowse and his wife, Mary. Their recorded occupation in 1901 was 'the fur toy business', which probably means the girls worked on the factory floor, making the high-class toys that found their way into the homes of the well-to-do. In 1905 Minnie was married and subsequently left Farnell but Jessie stayed on and, like Alice Upstone, became a trusted employee, particularly favoured by Agnes. As for male employees, it is widely believed that a man called Harry G Stone was working for Farnell at this time. The precise nature of Stone's duties is not known but he is thought to have been involved in the design and manufacturing processes rather than sales and marketing. He is a significant character because after he left Farnell he teamed up with Leon Rees of the Chiltern Toy Works in Chesham, Buckinghamshire. The pair opened a new factory in north London and quickly established themselves as close competitors of Farnell.

Recognising early Farnell teddy bears

While identifying Farnell's very first soft toys is virtually impossible, luckily there is much more clarity when it comes to their early teddy bears. First of all, there is the information found in the two Harrods catalogues of 1910. In each catalogue a photographic image of the bear referred to as TY 365 was used; helpfully, the photos were taken from different angles, making it easy to establish a clear three-dimensional idea of what the teddies looked like. Thanks to their filling of wood wool (the name given to the fine wood shavings used to stuff early soft toys) they were solid, substantial bears, and they had long arms which curved at the paw and long legs ending in cardboard-lined feet. Only the larger sizes featured the distinctive webbed claw stitching. The general shape of the bears was similar to their German counterparts, with long muzzles – often shaved, as in the case of TY 365 – and backs with rounded humps. By using a magnifying glass, it can be seen that the bear in the photo had glass eyes, which means it was one of the larger models, as Farnell were using shiny black boot buttons for their smaller teddies at this time. The nose stitching was vertical. From the catalogue descriptions we know that the bears were made from superior plush, came in nine different sizes and were fitted with a growl. Sadly the Harrods catalogues do not specify the colours of the 'superior plush' the bears were made from but Farnell teddies dating from around 1909 to 1920 are often found in white, blonde, light golden and golden shades of mohair. During this era the company also made bears in red, blue and black mohair, but today examples in these colours are rare and hard to come by.

Other clues to the appearance of early Farnell bears can be found in old postcards and photographs. In an age when not every family possessed its own camera, children routinely sat for studio portraits. Thanks to the overwhelming popularity of teddy bears, they frequently appeared in these photographs with their little owners. Postcard publishers also cashed in on the teddy bear's marketability by producing many cards featuring teddies in cute anthropomorphic situations. Although the identity of the bears' manufacturer was never indicated on these photos and postcards, some are instantly recognisable. For example, the teddy featured on a birthday postcard sent to a Miss A Gage in June 1915 has a very strong resemblance to TY 365. The bear, which has been dressed in bonnet and apron, is standing between two wicker cradles in which kittens are sleeping, with one paw resting on the top of a cradle. At this angle the webbed claw stitching is clearly visible, identifying the bear as a Farnell product. This is a rare stroke of luck, but even when the claw stitching is not visible it is possible to make an informed guess at a bear's identity, as with the large bear photographed sitting on the lap of a curly-haired mite. It has many of the characteristics of an early Farnell teddy and, while there is not enough evidence for absolute certainty, it may well be one.

There has been so much social and technological change in the last hundred years that today the era immediately preceding and following the First World War seems light years away. In terms of family history, however, it is not that long ago

Sent to Miss A Gage in 1915, this birthday card has a picture of a Farnell bear on the front.

and many people living today have memories of elderly relatives who were children when the teddy bear itself was young. Their recollections can be very helpful in identifying and learning about old Farnell teddies. From time to time examples turn up at auction accompanied by photos of their original owners, written or verbal accounts of their early years and other pieces of provenance. One such bear was offered for sale at Christie's South Kensington in December 2005. Known as 'Olive's Teddy Bear', it was a blonde Farnell measuring 19 inches high. According to the provenance, it had been given to Miss Olive Mary Round MBE when she was aged about four; since Miss Round was born in 1904, this information dated the bear to circa 1908–1909. Verbal provenance has been known to be flawed – people can be mistaken about dates or, very occasionally, they can make claims to enhance a bear's value – but that was not the case with 'Olive's Teddy Bear', which looked exactly as a Farnell bear dating from this era would be expected to look.

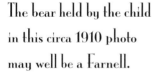

The bear held by the child in this circa 1910 photo may well be a Farnell.

Although he has had some restoration, this circa First World War Farnell teddy retains his original glass eyes, which are painted on the backs, and his nose and mouth stitching are also original.

Another early Farnell teddy with known provenance is that belonging to Kim Brittle from Essex. Kim's Aunt Edna was given Edbert when she was born in 1918 and Kim inherited Edbert in 2007 when her aunt died. Although Edbert is now, as Kim describes him, 'a little battle worn', his problems are fairly superficial. This was a bear that was played with and loved, not shoved in a cupboard and forgotten about, so a degree of wear and tear is to be expected. Edbert has suffered some fur loss over the years but the mohair that remains is long, thick and

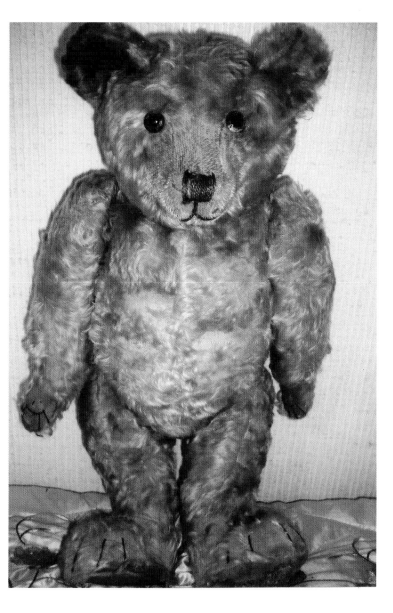

Edbert, the 1918 Farnell teddy owned by Kim Brittle's Aunt Edna.

lustrous, bearing testament to the exceptional quality of the mohair plush used by Farnell. Perhaps it was this wonderful mohair that caught the attention of a fashionable young mother when, in 1921, she went shopping in Harrods in search of a teddy bear for her son's first birthday. The mother was Daphne Milne, wife of the playwright Alan Alexander Milne, and within a few short years the Farnell bear she bought for her son Christopher Robin would become immortalised as Winnie the Pooh. (See Chapter 8 for the full story.)

Chapter 4

Perfection in Toys (1921–1930)

In 1921, the Farnell family decided to put the organisational structure of their company on a more formal footing. Since the death of their father, the siblings had effectively been operating as joint partners in the business although records show that, officially at least, only Henry Kirby was actively involved in the running of the company. This state of affairs may have changed during the war years when a shortage of men possibly encouraged the sisters to take a more hands-on approach. In any case, in October 1921 Henry Kirby Farnell, Eleanor Farnell, Agnes Farnell and Martha Monement 'sold' their toy business to a newly formed private limited company called J K Farnell & Co Ltd. Documentation held by Companies House shows that this new company was formed by Henry Kirby and Agnes Farnell, and while all four siblings became major shareholders in the company, owning 1,650 shares each, only Henry Kirby and Agnes were named as company directors. This is significant as it is the first occasion on which Agnes's name is formally associated with the business.

Two other individuals were also named as directors – Albert E B Rose and Frederick Harold Sully – and both became minor shareholders, owning a hundred shares apiece. Sully, a chartered accountant, does not appear to have had a personal connection with the Farnell family but Rose most certainly did. His father, Samuel Rose, was a schoolmaster who was teaching in Yorkshire when his wife Elizabeth gave birth to Albert in 1883. However, both parents originally came from London, and by the time Albert was seven the family (the Roses had two older children, Percy and Maud) had returned to their roots, settling in the Acton area. After leaving school Albert took a job as a bank clerk and by 1909 felt sufficiently confident of his future prospects to marry his fiancée. The girl in question was a certain Frances Monement, only child of Martha Monement and eldest grandchild of Joseph Kirby Farnell. By making Rose a director of the family business, the older Farnells were taking the first step towards passing their father's legacy on to the younger generation in due course.

In the newly established company's Memorandum of Association, its stated objectives were to

design, manufacture, make, construct, repair, alter, adapt, buy, sell, exchange, import, export and deal in toys, games, amusements, dolls, playthings and fancy goods of all kinds, in velvet, wool, plush, fur, skin, cotton, metal, celluloid, rubber, wood, cardboard, paper or any material whatsoever.

Furthermore, the company was to

carry on all or any such business as aforesaid and whether as wholesaler, retailer, agents or dealers or in any other manner whatsoever

and to

purchase or by any other means acquire any freehold, leasehold or other property for any estate or interest whatever, and any rights, property and any real or personal property or rights whatsoever which may be necessary for, or may be conveniently used with, or may enhance the value of any other property of the company.

It is quite a mouthful, but despite the convoluted legal language, the message is very clear – this is an ambitious company that is not going to be restricted in its trading options or the materials from which its products are manufactured, and future expansion is very much on the cards.

The firm's sound financial standing at the time of its incorporation as a private limited company is revealed in documentation held by Companies House. Its business assets, a term which probably encompassed premises, machinery, tools etc, were valued at £10,804 (£369,768 in modern money terms*) while the company's stock and cash was worth £10,404 (£356,078 today*). This very healthy state of affairs is quite remarkable considering the general state of British industry after the war. Many companies were feeling the pinch and the economic conditions might well have had a negative impact on Farnell since, as manufacturers of high-quality products made from the best raw materials, their

*Using figures from www.moneysorter.co.uk

toys were not cheap. Before the war the firm's prices were comparable with those commanded by Steiff, another top manufacturer with a reputation for excellence. After the war, however, this situation altered dramatically in favour of the German toy manufacturers. In an attempt to assist the rebuilding of the shattered German economy, the British government lifted the ban on German imports. This put pressure on the British teddy companies as they fought to retain their share of the domestic market, and things soon became much worse when the German currency collapsed. Having lost the Great War, Germany was obliged to make huge reparation payments to the Allies and the strain of doing so caused the

This fine Alpha Bear resides in the Puppenhausmuseum in Basel; it measures 45cm high and is made of golden mohair.

German mark to devalue, to such an extent that there were reports of women taking pram loads of bank notes to the shops in order to buy a single loaf of bread. Dire as the situation was for the German people, it proved advantageous to German manufacturers exporting their products to Britain. To put what this meant for Farnell into perspective, whereas before the war prices for their bears were on level pegging with similar German-made products, now the German bears might cost fifty per cent less. In Farnell's favour was the anti-German feeling that permeated parts of British society immediately after the war, although as retailers were not obliged to declare where their products came from, customers would only discover that the teddy they were buying had originated in Germany by asking a direct question. Despite the stiff competition, however, Farnell not only survived the 1920s but in fact positively flourished throughout the decade. This rapid growth was due to the excellence of its products, the ambitious expansion plans of its management team and the sharp rise in demand for high-quality soft toys. At the start of the 1920s, Farnell toys were being stocked by leading department stores such as Harrods and Dickens & Jones. The elite classes had always valued the firm's products but now ordinary members of the public were beginning to appreciate the difference between shoddy toys made from cheap materials and high-quality ones manufactured carefully from the best Yorkshire mohair or purest alpaca plush. Farnell's refusal to compromise on quality was entirely in tune with the mood of the age.

'I Am The Alpha Bear' advertisement from Games and Toys, February 1922.

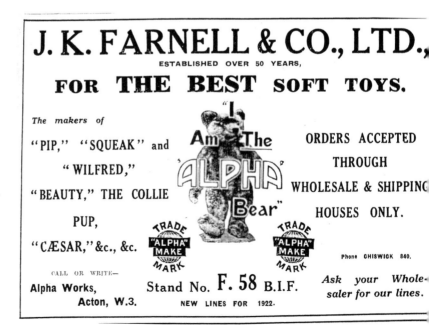

J. K. FARNELL & CO., LTD.,

ESTABLISHED OVER 50 YEARS,

FOR THE BEST SOFT TOYS.

The makers of

"PIP," "SQUEAK" and "WILFRED,"

"BEAUTY," THE COLLIE PUP,

"CÆSAR," &c., &c.

"I Am The ALPHA Bear"

TRADE "ALPHA" MAKE MARK

TRADE "ALPHA" MAKE MARK

ORDERS ACCEPTED THROUGH WHOLESALE & SHIPPING HOUSES ONLY.

Phone CHISWICK 840.

CALL OR WRITE—

Alpha Works, Acton, W.3.

Stand No. F. 58 B.I.F.

NEW LINES FOR 1922.

Ask your Wholesaler for our lines.

Alpha, miniature, Silkalite and other bears

In February 1922, the toy trade journal *Games and Toys* wrote about Farnell's 'Alpha' series of soft toys. 'The workmanship of this firm's specialities is too well known for us to comment upon,' the article ran, 'and they justly occupy premier place amongst the manufacturers today.' In an advertisement accompanying the article, Farnell made mention of several soft toy animals including Pip, Squeak and Wilfred, characters – respectively a dog, penguin and young rabbit – from the *Daily Mirror*'s highly successful cartoon strip, which was first published in 1919. However, the only product illustrated in the advertisement is a magnificent teddy bear, which is depicted as if striding purposefully forwards. Super-imposed over this illustration are the words 'I Am The Alpha Bear.' The words and imagery used in the advert exemplify the pride Farnell felt in their teddy bears; this, they were saying, is the best teddy bear on the market. Far from being an idle boast, it

'Perfection In Toys' advertisement from June 1925.

Tiny bears and other animals were big news in 1925.

was a view shared by many, sometimes to the detriment of Farnell because unscrupulous competitors were not above attempting to pass their own bears off as Farnell products.

Although imitation is often said to be the sincerest form of flattery, Farnell decided that action needed to be taken when imitation resulted in loss of business. Early attempts to trademark their products had not been entirely successful. In the *Games and Toys* advertisement of February 1922, for example, two identical 'trademark' logos appeared, in the shape of globes, which had the words 'Alpha Make' printed across the middle and around which the words Trade Mark appeared. Nevertheless, as late as June 1925, cases were still being reported of inferior products being substituted for genuine Farnell toys. To combat this, the company officially registered its trademark that year and thereafter all its bears and other toys left the factory with a sewn-on Farnell cloth label. While the trademark's registration date is known to be 1925, precisely when Farnell began using the Alpha trade name is less clear, but it was probably around 1921, the same time that the firm became a private limited company. This was also when the Farnell factory premises began to be referred to as the Alpha Works; prior to this the company's address was listed simply as The Elms, Acton Hill, W3. Even after 1921, although the Alpha Works name was lodged with Companies House and was being quoted in trade advertisements, it did not make it into the regional telephone directory until 1926. It has been claimed that the Alpha Works was a brand new factory complex, built alongside the existing factory in order to cope with increased demand, and this may indeed be the case although it has not been possible to find evidence to support the idea.

The confidence displayed by Farnell in the 1922 'I Am The Alpha Bear' advertisement was an early taste of what was to come as the company grew in confidence and developed greater awareness of the power of marketing. In June 1925, an advertisement showing a number of toys including a sitting teddy bear appeared in the trade press with the caption 'Perfection In Toys' printed above the picture. Gone was any residual reticence about self-promotion, replaced from now on by increasingly bullish advertising campaigns which were backed up by almost reverential editorial from the trade journals. Undoubtedly the new tone of the advertising was the result of overwhelming enthusiasm for Farnell's products. Alongside the Alpha Bear – a solid, very traditionally shaped mohair teddy with long arms, strapping thighs and a vertically stitched nose – were bears in a wide

A 21-inch white mohair Farnell bear – the noses and mouths of white bears were
stitched in brown thread.

variety of sizes and styles, including a diminutive example launched in 1925 as part of a range of miniature animals. Measuring no more than 3.5 inches high, the little bear had a retail price of a shilling, giving – in the words of *Games and Toys* – 'a good margin of profit to both wholesaler and retailer'. As well as the tiny teddy, unjointed pandas made from black and white mohair were also available in the range. They were made in at least two sizes – 4 and 5 inches – and had brown and black glass eyes which were backed with black felt. A light-coloured bear standing on all fours was also offered in the miniature range. So popular did this line prove that considerable quantities were shipped to Germany, a case of 'coals to Newcastle' according to the consistently enthusiastic *Games and Toys*.

In 1927 Farnell introduced a new line called the Anima Wheel Toys, which stood out from more run-of-the-mill wheeled toys as they were made from best-quality

ALL-BRITISH   "SILKALITE"
                      BEAR

VISIT STAND D 3 B.I.F.

J. K. FARNELL & CO., LTD.
ALPHA WORKS, ACTON HILL, LONDON, W. 3
Telephone—Chiswick 0840.   Telegrams—"Alphatoiz, Act, London."
London Showrooms—19, NEW UNION STREET, MOORGATE, E.C.2
Telephone—London Wall 7113
THE J. K. FARNELL & Co., Ltd. DEPT. of LOUIS WOLF & Co., Inc.
215-219, Fourth Avenue, New York.
SOCIÉTÉ ANONYME J. K. FARNELL. 80. Rue du Faubourg St-Denis. Paris.

In 1929 Farnell launched their Silkalite Bear, made from artificial silk plush.

While brightly coloured bears were fashionable in the 1920s, this example with black, silver-tipped mohair is a rarity.

long pile plush rather than the natural skins or short plush more commonly used. The advantage the new Anima toys had over their competition was that the long pile was far more cuddly to the touch, making the toys more appealing to their target market. Although toys representing different breeds of dogs were all the rage at this time, Farnell did not neglect to include a bear in the Anima range, thereby showing greater foresight than the journalist who wrote in *Games and Toys* in February 1929 that 'The day of the teddy bear is on the wane, and it has been succeeded by dogs.' While Farnell enthusiastically embraced the craze for cute dogs and puppies, it remained faithful to teddy bears, continuing even at the height of the 'dog years' to produce a great variety of them. A visitor to Farnell's city showrooms in July 1928 recorded seeing a 'wonderful range of teddy bears in a variety of colours. These included gold, white, mauve, blue, red, green and orange.' Filled with wood wool – fine wood shavings – or kapok according to price, the teddies filled the visitor with admiration, leaving 'no doubt as to the quality, finish and appearance of these bears'. A few of these colourful bears would probably have been part of a range made especially for infants; they were unjointed, measured about 10 inches high and had paw pads made from brushed cotton. Examples have been found in blue mohair so it seems likely that pink mohair was also used to conform to the stereotypical 'blue for a boy, pink for a girl'. Just over six months later, Farnell were advertising their new Silkalite Bear, a teddy not unlike the Alpha Bear in appearance but made from an exciting new synthetic material described as 'a beautiful artificial silk plush' instead of Yorkshire mohair. Silkalite proved popular with buyers because of its novelty value and also because it lent itself to fashionable colours more readily than mohair. When other manufacturers began making bears from artificial silk plush, they charged more for them than for mohair teddies, but with an eye to staying ahead in what was swiftly to become a difficult market place, Farnell sold its Silkalite Bear 'at the ordinary teddy bear price'. This instinct for surviving in a troubled economic climate was soon to stand Farnell in good stead when, following the Wall Street Crash of October 1929, the world economy went into freefall.

New faces

The burgeoning, increasingly competitive soft toy industry of the 1920s was very different from the fledgling industry the Farnell family had stumbled into back in

Striking Farnell teddy from the late 1920s
made from mohair in a vibrant turquoise shade.

Rare silver–grey Silkalite Bear.

the 1860s. The market had grown and the way in which business was conducted had altered too. Where previously the sheer novelty value of teddy bears and other soft toys had seen buyers beating a path to the doors of the few existing manufacturers, now new tactics such as aggressive advertising and marketing were necessary if the company was to stay afloat. The older Farnells may well have felt out of place in the new environment; after all, they had been born in the middle of the nineteenth century and quite apart from the fact that they were now rather elderly, their Victorian values would have been at odds with the times. Fortunately, elderly or not, the children of Joseph Kirby Farnell were still attuned to the needs of their business, realising that it was no longer sufficient for J K Farnell & Co Ltd to rest on its laurels as the premier British soft toy manufacturer. They knew that in order for their company to survive, it needed to sharpen up. Accordingly, one of their first steps was to secure the services of Henry Clarence Janisch, a young man in his mid-to-late twenties who was more in tune with the mood of the era. An accomplished sales professional, Janisch brought a much-needed touch of modernity to Farnell. The year he joined the company is not known but he was already there in 1922 when he represented Farnell at a Board of Trade inquiry concerning allegations of unfair competition from German manufacturers. During the inquiry, he alleged – according to Kenneth D Brown's *The British Toy*

ALPHA.
MR. J. K. JANISCH.

Cartoon by 'Mac' of Henry Clarence Janisch, 1926.

Business – that a group of German makers had pledged to break the British manufacturers. Whether true or not, the breadth of the allegation and the fact that Farnell chose him to represent their interests suggests Janisch must already have had considerable experience in the toy trade. Unfortunately for Farnell, Janisch's skills made him an attractive prospect for other manufacturers and at the end of the decade he was lured away to help launch a brand new soft toy manufacturing company called Merrythought.

Another experienced toy professional who brought valuable insight and expertise to Farnell in the 1920s was Thomas Wright – more usually known as T B Wright – who joined in March 1926. Before that, he had worked for seventeen years as 'ambassador-in-chief' for a well-known American agent, W E Peck and Co Ltd. Despite this rather grand (if ambiguous-sounding) job title, with Farnell Wright worked as a sales representative reporting to Janisch. Sometime around 1928 or 1929, increased volume of business necessitated the employment of two additional sales representatives, Henry E Williams and a Mr Leonard. However, while the new staff brought fresh energy and ideas to J K Farnell & Co Ltd, the family members were not yet prepared to step back from the business their father had established. Agnes kept a sufficiently close eye on things to be on friendly terms with the girls on the shop floor and Henry Kirby's involvement in the day-to-day affairs of the company meant he needed a private office within the factory premises. Additionally, sometime during the 1920s Albert E B Rose, husband of Joseph Kirby Farnell's granddaughter Frances, became heavily involved in the running of the company, becoming its chairman by 1929 at the latest. As for the hundreds of other people known to have been working for the company during the 1920s, only two can be identified for certain – Sybil Kemp and Jessie Prowse, both of whom had been employed by Farnell since 1900 or thereabouts. As has been previously stated, there is a verbal tradition that Sybil Kemp's duties involved designing teddy bears for Farnell. While there is no firm evidence to support this, at least one designer of the period can be positively identified. Chloe Preston worked for the company on a freelance basis, designing toys that proved hugely popular and contributed to Farnell's business boom. A popular children's illustrator, Preston began her successful association with Farnell in 1925, but although she designed a number of memorable dogs, cats and dolls (see Chapter 7) she does not appear to have turned her hand to teddy bears.

Extension, expansion and innovation

With a crack sales team in place, Farnell was ready to embark on an ambitious programme of expansion. In 1927, a new wing of 7,000 square feet capable of holding several hundred workers was built, this in addition to the existing factory building, which already gave employment to hundreds. The extension was needed to manage the greatly increased demand for Farnell's Alpha toys. One year later the company opened its first ever showroom, which was based in New Union Street, EC2. Prior to the establishment of the City showroom, the only opportunities for trade buyers to view Farnell's teddies and toys outside its factory premises had been at the annual British Industries Fair held in White City, London every February, or at 'special shows' staged at large hotels. As with the

A Farnell workroom in 1929. The conditions are good for the era with plenty of space and light.

Although he has lost mohair from his chest and his nose has been restitched, this 15-inch, golden mohair teddy from the 1920s is otherwise in good condition.

factory extension, the need for the City showroom arose from a huge increase in business. 'Shipping business' – export, in other words – was on the up, as were domestic orders, following Farnell's decision to start selling directly to the retail trade where previously they had restricted themselves to wholesalers. With a new, centrally located showroom, the company had a prestigious location in which to meet with the new influx of buyers from home and abroad.

The showroom consisted of one large floor which was divided into sections showcasing the firm's various toys, with private offices at the rear. It was a light, airy space with the toys displayed on open shelving, in glass cabinets and even on the floor, in the case of the largest soft toys and the Anima wheeled range. According to *Games and Toys*, the toys were 'displayed to the best possible advantage, not overcrowded' with 'each class of toy is in its own particular group'. Although dogs were prominently displayed throughout the showroom, 1928 being one of the years in which the craze for toy dogs was at its height, teddy bears were also very much in evidence. The showroom was manned by Mr Leonard, designated the London representative, and also occasionally by T B Wright, although he was more usually to be found promoting Farnell's toys in provincial towns and cities.

With operations on very solid ground at home, in 1929 the company launched itself on to the international marketplace with the formation of two separate organisations based in different parts of the world. In the lucrative North American market, a collaboration between Farnell and Louis Wolf and Co resulted in the formation of the cumbersome-sounding 'The J K Farnell & Co Ltd, Department of Louis Wolf and Co Inc', with a showroom situated at Fourth Avenue, New York. To strengthen Farnell's chances of capturing the goodwill of North American toy buyers, company chairman Albert Brett Rose set off on an extensive tour of the USA and Canada. At the same time a new company was established much closer to home with the aim of capitalising on the strong interest Farnell had been seeing from buyers in France, Belgium and Switzerland. Based in Paris at Rue du Fauborg St Denis, the 'Société Anonyme J K Farnell' occupied extensive showrooms displaying a complete range of the company's products. Nor was this the full extent of Farnell's ambition: having conquered Britain and made inroads into North America and French-speaking Europe, the company now turned its attention to Central Europe. Spearheading this audacious onslaught on

Section of the stuffing room.

a market that was already well served by its native manufacturers was Joseph Susskind, a well-respected figure in the German toy trade with whom Farnell had been associated for thirty years. Exporting soft toys to Germany could have been regarded as another classic example of 'coals to Newcastle' but according to *Games and Toys* the move was justified because there was 'a large demand in Germany for this firm's goods, due to their unequalled quality and originality'.

With a view to expanding into these new markets, Farnell embarked on a programme of exhibiting at prestigious overseas trade fairs. This was an astute and somewhat radical step for a British company because at the time most UK manufacturers showed a marked reluctance to step outside the comfort zone of the domestic exhibition scene. In 1926, when Farnell exhibited at the world's leading trade fair in Leipzig, it was one of only thirteen British companies to do so. Three years later, in order to gain ground in the USA, Farnell added New York and Chicago to its trade fair itinerary, which already included Leipzig and London.

Other innovative tactics employed by Farnell during the 1920s included trade circulars, expensive advertisements in national newspapers such as the *Daily Mail* and, in 1929, the introduction of a colour catalogue, which was made available to 'every retailer and draper in the country'. The impact the colour catalogue had on the toy trade should not be underestimated; at the time, it was regarded almost as an act of genius. In the February 1930 edition of *Games and Toys*, a somewhat breathless article entitled 'A Catalogue Par Excellence' extolled the catalogue's virtues over two full pages. Having paid tribute to Farnell for being the first toy manufacturer to produce a colour catalogue, one 'accurately portraying the actual toys they manufacture', the article goes on to describe the forty-eight-page catalogue of 1930 as 'a revelation of not only the wonderful toys which Farnell's place on the market, but also a revelation of the excellence which the printing trade in this country can put out. In both these directions', the writer patriotically asserted, 'we stand second to none in the world.' The artificial silk Silkalite bear featured prominently in the catalogue. Sadly, Farnell catalogues today are as rare as the proverbial hen's teeth, and it has not been possible to locate a copy of the 'really handsome production' that created such a stir in 1930, although sections from a catalogue published just a few years later are reproduced in chapters 5 and 6.

The Farnell factory floor

The company's policy of paying high wages – eighty per cent higher than the rate suggested by the Board of Trade in 1928, with performance bonuses of up to fifteen per cent of earnings – resulted in a happy workforce dedicated to upholding the high standards of their employer. In 1929, Farnell needed between five and six hundred employees in order to keep pace with demand, and thanks to the firm's good working conditions local people were so eager to fill their vacancies that a waiting list was kept. When new positions became available workers from the waiting list were hired on a trial basis and then tried out at the various processes until they found one to which they were suited. If that did not happen, they were replaced. Photographs of the factory at this time show rows of women in large, airy workrooms sitting on wooden chairs with their work in front of them on long, trestle-type tables. Baskets of fabric lie on the floor behind the workers' chairs and shelves filled with plush and completed toys are dotted about the room. There is plenty of space around the tables and as far as can be judged from a photograph the women look happy and the atmosphere congenial.

Till death do us part

The 1920s started on a promising note for the Farnell family with the marriage in February 1920 of Beatrice, Charles Burcham Farnell's second daughter, to a man called Allatt Henry Hollins. (Charles Burcham had died in Norfolk in 1918; it is not known if he was in contact with his family at the time of his death.) The son of a 'grey cloth merchant', Allatt Hollins was born in Cheshire in 1895 and served as a Lieutenant in the Duke of Cornwall's Light Infantry during the First World War. He would have been nineteen when the war broke out, one of the generation of young men hurled abruptly from a carefree youth into the horrors of war. Beatrice was either engaged to Hollins before he went to war or they met and fell in love whilst he was on leave, because he returned home from Nigeria in December 1919 and their marriage took place at the beginning of 1920. Hollins was a professional soldier and he spent time in India in the early 1920s. Whether Beatrice accompanied him is unclear but at home in the UK their address was The Elms, Acton. They were to have three children, Rosemary, Jane and Timothy, all of whom were to become shareholders in the family firm at a later date.

Three years after Beatrice's marriage, her Aunt Eleanor, the oldest surviving child of Joseph Kirby Farnell, died, aged seventy-seven. She was buried in North Acton Cemetery. Then, in October 1927, an event occurred that may have surprised many who knew the family. At the age of forty-two, Mary Farnell – the oldest daughter of Charles Burcham – married Richard Williams, a doctor from Acton with connections in Eastbourne. Williams may have been the Farnells' doctor; Agnes certainly knew and liked him because he was named in her will, which was written before his marriage to her niece. (It is tempting to suppose there may have been some connection between Dr Richard Williams and the Henry Williams who joined Farnell in the late 1920s; he may, for instance, have been a son from a previous marriage. While this is no more than speculation – Williams is, after all, a not uncommon surname – it could explain why Henry Williams rose to a position of prominence in the company, ultimately becoming a director and token shareholder.) The newlyweds set up home in Gunnersbury Avenue, Ealing, within easy distance of the bride's family at The Elms and the Farnell factory.

On 25 January 1928, just over three months after Mary's marriage, Agnes Farnell died at home at The Elms in her seventy-seventh year. She was laid to rest with her sister Eleanor in North Acton Cemetery. Although she had never

Piles of toys await final assembly in the finishing room.

married, Agnes had lived a full life, keeping house for her father when her mother died, raising her estranged brother's daughters, and helping to create the dynamic company that J K Farnell & Co Ltd undoubtedly was in the 1920s. Her will reveals that she had made some lifelong friends amongst the employees of the company, notably Alice Upstone, who was left a legacy of £50 and was named as one of her three executors and trustees. Sybil Kemp and Jessie Prowse were left a similar legacy, as were Farnell directors Frederick Sully and Albert Rose, who were named alongside Alice Upstone as co-executors and trustees. The will demonstrates clearly that there were two strong influences in Agnes Farnell's life – her business and her family. Although all three of her nieces were named in her will, the two for whom she had acted as a surrogate mother received the bulk of her considerable estate (its gross value was £12,246 which in today's money would be worth around £537,000), with Mary – an unmarried woman when the will was written, although not when Agnes died – doing best of all. Her sister Martha was mentioned in passing but did not receive a legacy and her brother, Henry Kirby, was named as the beneficiary of a trust fund that Agnes required her trustees to set up after her death. Now of the seven children known to have been born to Joseph Kirby and Elizabeth Farnell, only Martha and Henry Kirby remained, survivors of a swiftly vanishing world.

The 1920s drew to a close with another death in the family. At the end of October 1929, Frances Marguerite Rose, Martha Monement's only child, died at the age of just forty-six. The cause of her death, certified by her cousin-in-law Richard Williams, was carcinoma of the mediastinum (the part of the thoracic cavity that contains the heart), leading to lung collapse and heart failure. The premature death of her only child must have been a crushing blow for Martha, who does not seem to have had much happiness in her life, and it was no less of a blow for Albert E B Rose, who described his wife in the death notice he placed in *The Times* as 'beloved and devoted', suggesting theirs had been a happy marriage. With Frances gone, Rose now became a very eligible widower.

The Farnell Wagon

In May 1926, a general strike called by the trade unions in support of coal miners' wages and working conditions threatened to bring the country to its knees. The strike lasted ten days, from 3–13 May, but its impact was never as great as the politicians and press of the day had feared. However, as the railway and transport workers came out on strike, getting to work was a challenge for anyone who didn't live within walking distance of their employment. With their output dependent on the labour of hundreds of employees, mostly women, Farnell could not afford to have its workforce languishing at home, so the company hit on an ingenious solution to the transport problem. They hired a 'pantechnicon', fitted it with seats and obtained a Fordson tractor to pull it along. The 'Farnell Wagon', as it came to be known, was one of the sights of the general strike in the Acton area.

Chapter 5

Achievement at the House of Farnell

(1931–1940)

T he 1930s were to present Farnell with a number of challenges, most of which were shared by their competitors, but there was one – and it was a major challenge – that was all their own. Had the company not been in such splendid shape thanks to the expansion and boom it had experienced in the 1920s, it may have struggled to survive. However, with a solid organisational infrastructure, a healthy balance book and an undiminished reputation for excellence, the company was able to ride out the coming storm and even, amazingly, forge ahead with further expansion. All the same, those with a vested interest in the House of Farnell – as the trade press took to calling it in the 1930s – must have spent some sleepless nights during the early part of the decade.

The biggest problem besetting Farnell and every other commercial organisation in the early 1930s was the severely depressed economy which immediately followed the Wall Street Crash of October 1929. The collapse of the New York stock market sent shock waves around the world as millions of dollars were wiped off share values. Many formerly wealthy people found they had lost everything and the knock-on effect filtered down into the lives of ordinary men and women. Although the Crash happened in the USA, its repercussions were felt all over the world. In Britain, the crisis led to the fall of the country's first Labour government, followed by the formation of a national coalition government made up of all three major parties, with Ramsay MacDonald remaining Prime Minister.

For heavy industry such as ship building, steel and coal mining the consequences of the Crash were very severe and unemployment soared, rising from 1.5 million in January 1930 to nearly 3 million in January 1933. Life for those without work could be very grim because even though unemployment benefit did exist it was scarcely enough to support a family. When the government was forced to cut benefit by ten per cent in 1931, things became even harder. Even for those still employed, however, life could be a struggle since low wages meant there was seldom enough money even for the basics. In such times, when many families were struggling simply to survive, it was inevitable that things would become difficult for the toy industry. After all, given the choice of putting food on the table or buying, say, a teddy bear, only a madman would opt for the latter. As a result, manufacturers, wholesalers and retailers all saw their profits slump and indeed some were unable to keep their heads above water.

The Cheapest Soft Toys in the World

Farnell's answer to the problem was characteristically bold. Far from reducing production, cutting overheads and waiting patiently for the economy to pick up, a strategy that the company was financially stable enough to follow, they decided to introduce a brand new line of cheap soft toys to be sold alongside their more expensive Alpha range. Launched in January 1931, the new range was called Unicorn Soft Toys, with a logo, appropriately enough, of a handsome prancing unicorn. Dogs featured heavily in the Unicorn range but as tried and trusted sellers teddy bears were also included. It was a new departure for Farnell to be marketing cut-price products and the company, anxious to protect its reputation for excellence, went to immense pains to convince potential buyers that their high standards were not compromised when manufacturing these cheaper toys. No doubt at Farnell's suggestion, the trade press ran articles explaining that the surprisingly low prices were made possible by Farnell's high turnover, which kept their overheads correspondingly low.

Described by Farnell in their advertisements as 'The Cheapest Soft Toys in the World', the whole point of the Unicorn range was to attract large orders from the sort of wholesalers who would ordinarily buy foreign imports, which tended to be less expensive than British-made toys. These wholesalers supplied the retail outlets frequented by people on lower incomes for whom Farnell's Alpha Toys were out of reach. Thus, with the Unicorn range the plan was to grab a sizeable share of the mass market by offering quality, affordable toys. Prices – euphemistically referred to as 'popular' – started at one shilling and many items cost no more than five shillings, but even where higher prices were charged the toys still represented unusual value for money. To make the Unicorn products even more attractive to the wholesalers, Farnell made them unavailable to retailers, so any shop wishing to stock them had to obtain them via a wholesaler. Furthermore, the company undertook to publish in the trade press on a monthly basis a countrywide list of the wholesalers carrying the range, so every toy retailer would know where to go to obtain stock. As a final carrot, Farnell promised to provide every wholesaler with as many free illustrated catalogues as they needed to give to their customers in order to promote the range, with a blank space on the front of each catalogue for the name and address of the wholesaler.

It proved to be a brilliant and highly successful strategy, one that perfectly illustrates the reason for Farnell's pre-eminence in the soft toy world at this time. By analysing the state of the market and identifying an opportunity to grow the business, the directors showed great commercial acumen, but their real achievement lay in having the courage to take a substantial risk in a depressed economy. Within twelve months, the gambit had paid off beyond all reasonable expectations. As new director Gerald E Beer revealed in an article in the February 1932 issue of *Games and Toys*, half a million Unicorn toys had been sold in the British Isles in 1931. As Beer commented, this was the first time Farnell had ever publicised such sales figures and the company's motivation in doing so now was to convince the sceptical that British manufacturers – notably Farnell themselves – could compete with foreign producers. Astoundingly, given the success of the Unicorn range, Beer described 1931 as 'admittedly a difficult year' but the adjective was no doubt intended to refer to the general state of the economy rather than to the state of Farnell's order book. In the same paragraph he announced Farnell's plans to extend considerably the Unicorn range although only items considered 'safe' would be included. 'Safe' was a euphemism for 'guaranteed to sell', so the perennially popular teddy bear remained in the range, which once again featured enough dogs to rival the Kennel Club.

Predictably, Farnell's success with the Unicorn range encouraged other less pioneering manufacturers blatantly to rip off their most popular designs, even to the extent of attaching to their fake copies red, white and blue labels similar to those used on genuine Unicorn toys. Farnell reported receiving complaints from

THE CHEAPEST QUALITY SOFT TOYS IN THE WORLD

UNICORN

"DUSTY"

✻

Write for Catalogue
to the Manufacturers

✻

J. K. FARNELL
& CO. LTD.

19 NEW UNION STREET, E.C.2
ALPHA WORKS, ACTON HILL, W.3

"The Season's
most popular
Toy"

Farnell advertised their Unicorn range as the cheapest quality soft toys in the world; in retrospect, a comma between 'cheapest' and 'quality' would have been advisable.

people who had bought the copies in the mistaken belief that they were genuine and were now dissatisfied with their poor quality. To clarify the situation, Farnell responded that the Unicorn trademark was registered and only items bearing tickets on which the Unicorn name was distinctly printed were genuine Farnell toys. This is just one example of how, for all the success of the Unicorn range, Farnell do not seem to have been entirely comfortable trading at the cheap end of the toy market. The company continued to reiterate that low prices were not inconsistent with high-quality products and, further, insisted that samples shown to prospective buyers at trade fairs were taken randomly from stock and were therefore truly representative of their output. They also asserted that all their products were checked twice before leaving the factory and 'should the millionth chance occur and a single item arrive that is not perfect the customer has only to return it at our expense'. The Farnell hierarchy probably imagined these comments were required in order to fight back against unjustified complaints but to modern sensibilities at least they perhaps strike an unnecessarily defensive note. Nevertheless, demand for the Unicorn range remained high and the following year (1933) the firm exhibited a number of additions to it on their stand at the Olympia trade fair. Once again, the familiar statement about high turnover enabling the company to retain excellent standards whilst offering low prices was trotted out, and the 'Cheapest Soft Toys in the World' slogan was still in use with one slight amendment – the word 'Quality' had been inserted between 'Cheapest' and 'Soft Toys'. An article published in the April 1933 issue of *Games and Toys* is revealing about the differences between Farnell's high-quality products and the inferior goods offered by certain other manufacturers. Thanks to a special arrangement with its mohair provider, the company was able to reserve 'special cloths and plushes' for

Fire at the Alpha Works, July 1934.

its exclusive use, enabling it to produce toys that no other firm could make. This, however, was only one part of the equation. Describing Farnell as 'artists in soft toy production', the article extolled their ability to blend colours so cleverly that remarkable effects were achieved. It was the writer's opinion that 'the blending of these colours for their products is perhaps one of the main reasons for the many successes in soft toy numbers they have introduced.'

Rising from the ashes

One summer's evening in 1934, everything Joseph Kirby Farnell and his successors had spent decades striving for was very nearly wiped out within a few minutes. Just before 7pm on Monday, 16 July, not long after the workforce had left for the evening, a fire took hold somewhere in the Alpha Works and spread rapidly to a quantity of inflammable material. Very soon the entire factory was ablaze – when the Acton fire brigade arrived, the fire had already spread from one end of the building to the other. In a desperate bid to save valuable stock, men and boys formed a cordon and passed boxes of toys and fabrics and threw them over a wall on to the lawn of The Elms. Thick crowds of onlookers threatened to impede the firemen who were concentrating on preventing the fire from spreading to The Elms, so boy scouts were used to control the crowds while the police let the fire-fighters through. According to newspaper reports, the heat from the flames was so intense that the firemen had to turn their hoses on each other, and even by the following morning they were still hosing the smouldering ruins of the building in order to prevent the fire from reigniting. The cause of the conflagration was not reported but there would have been plenty of fuel to feed the flames once they had taken hold. Great clumps of dust formed from kapok and wood wool used to gather around iron girders in the shed and these would have burned merrily in a fire. Whatever the cause of the disaster, the factory and everything inside it, including most of next season's stock, was completely destroyed, although by some miracle The Elms escaped with just slight damage at the rear, leaving Henry Kirby Farnell and Martha Monement with a roof over their heads even though their business was in ashes. The loss of the factory and its stock was a catastrophic blow, coming at a time when the company reportedly had 'more orders in hand than at any time in their long and honoured career'.

Such widespread destruction might have vanquished the spirit of a less resolute company, but not Farnell: while the trade press was still commiserating with the firm about the fire, the directors were calmly going about the business of rebuilding. So swift were they in getting started that the new premises were ready for occupation by the late spring of 1935, less than a year since the disaster. Fortunately for posterity, Albert E B Rose invited a writer from *Games and Toys* to tour the new factory and thus a detailed description of the premises was duly recorded. Built of 'solid brick', the square-shaped building occupied 23,000 square feet, and was very light due to parts of the roof being made of glass. 'The factory has been so designed', *Games and Toys* reported, 'and the departments for the various processes of manufacture placed in such a position that the flow of work from the receipt of the raw materials to the boxing and despatch of the finished article follows their natural sequence – thus making for considerable time-saving.'

At one end of the factory, large quantities of different types of plush were stacked on racks. To make a toy, first the pattern was marked out on to the appropriate plush, after which workers cut out the pieces by hand. Farnell were proud of the fact that their cutting was done by hand, claiming that only hand-cut material would give the best finish, and their cutters needed to be experienced since the high price of plush meant any mistakes could prove costly. Adjoining the cutting department was an area furnished with a number of electric sewing machines, and here the various toy parts were sewn together. Following the sewing, the operation moved to the stuffing department, and further on there was the area for fixing eyes into the toys' heads. A product's journey from uncut plush to huggable toy concluded in the finishing department, where ribbons were applied, whiskers trimmed, fur brushed and any other last-minute detail attended to before the item moved on to the nearby packing department. The offices of Henry Kirby Farnell and Albert E B Rose were located in another part of the factory, as was 'the counting house' – the old-fashioned name for the accounts office. Next to the offices was the designing room and both this and the offices had doors leading out to the main works.

With staff welfare in mind, the company had invested considerable sums in providing a comfortable and hygienic working environment. A clean, spacious kitchen complete with large gas stove was provided for the preparation of the employees' lunches, which were eaten in a canteen outside the main building. A rest room for senior workers was also provided, giving them a place in which to eat their meals away from the rest of the workforce or simply enjoy a brief nap. In order to keep the workers warm, a very large boiler and an electric pump were housed inside a brick-built outhouse, providing hot water that was pumped through pipes into radiators in the main building. The pipes were painted green and the walls cream, and in order to avoid another fire three coats of fireproof paint were applied. Although expensive, painting the walls was regarded as a hygiene-conscious measure, and the company was congratulated by factory inspectors for adopting the healthy practice.

The new factory was large enough to hold 300 employees, a far cry from the 500 or 600 required in 1929 to keep up with demand. However, within a couple of months the factory had been further extended to accommodate a section devoted to the manufacture of high-class dolls (see Chapter 7) and a completely new building was already under construction. By May 1937 a new wing had been erected in front of the whole length of the factory, providing a separate location for the stuffing department, stores and additional offices. The factory was now one of the largest soft toy works in the world. The lightning speed at which this feverish construction had taken place demonstrates Farnell's refusal to allow adversity to halt its expansion plans. The workforce required to staff the new building and the extensions would have taken the number of employees back to the level of 1929 and possibly even in excess of it. It was at this time that Farnell took to describing themselves in their advertising as 'The Oldest and Most Famous Soft Toy and Doll Manufacturers in the World'.

Bosses and bigwigs

In February 1937 *Games and Toys* ran a highly congratulatory three-and-a-half page article about J K Farnell & Co Ltd, using as a title for the piece just the one word: 'Achievement'. As the article's writer put it, through slumps and a fire the firm had reached the height of attainment. 'Here indeed is achievement,' the article declared, 'and the high position which they hold today in the soft toy industries of the world is undoubtedly due to the care, thought and attention to detail which the Managing Director, Mr A.E.B. Rose, has given during his association with this house.' There is no question that the praise was justified. Throughout the traumatic 1930s, Albert E B Rose fulfilled the joint roles of Chairman and Managing Director.

MR AE B. ROSE   OF J.K FARNELL

Says DUSTY took the biscuit

Cartoon of Albert E B
Rose by 'Mac', 1934.

As for Rose's fellow directors, he, Henry Kirby Farnell and Frederick Sully were joined on the board in 1930 by Mary Williams and Beatrice Hollins – the daughters of Charles Burcham Farnell – and Gerald Edward Beer. Through their Aunt Agnes's will both Mary and Beatrice had become substantial shareholders and they apparently wanted to have a say in how their company was run, unlike their surviving aunt, Martha Monement, who was never a director despite being a major shareholder. Beer, on the other hand, does not appear to have had a family connection with the Farnells. He was an ambitious thirty-two year old who had what looks like a fairly stormy relationship with Farnell; Company House records show that he resigned as a director in June 1932 but was reinstated in April 1934. In March 1936 he resigned again and this time his departure was permanent as he was now involved in the formation of a new toy company called Invicta Toys. His partner in the Invicta enterprise was Thomas Wright, who had been working with Farnell as a sales representative since 1926. The departure of Beer and Wright left the way clear for Harry Williams to climb higher in the Farnell hierarchy, although if he was related by marriage to Mary Williams (née Farnell) his career progression may in any case have been assured. Additional sales help came via an arrangement with Midlands toy company

William Bailey (Birmingham), which manufactured construction toys called Wenebrik and Kliptiko. As the two firms were addressing different sectors of the toy market, it was possible for one sales team to sell both companies' products, thus keeping staff overheads down. On the family front, the decade was less eventful than the one that had preceded it, although one occurrence of note was the remarriage of Albert E B Rose, in the summer of 1932, to a lady by the name of Ellen Baker.

Cheap Bear, Teddy Series and the return of the Alpha

At the start of the 1930s, although teddy bears were still popular, they were fighting a rearguard action against their canine rivals, which were everywhere at that time. For a short period, dogs probably usurped the teddy bear's premier position at Farnell; apart from a few casual references to teddies that come across almost as an afterthought, the only bear mentioned in any detail in the trade press during this time was the wheeled Anima. Even then, the bear was named last in a long list of twelve different Anima models, the majority of which, predictably enough, were various breeds of dog. Very soon, however, the pendulum was going to swing back in favour of the teddy bear.

At the Olympia trade show in 1933, Farnell introduced a new range of teddy bears which were strategically placed to interest the wholesale market. *Games and Toys* reported that these new bears represented remarkable value and that 'both the wholesaler and the retailer is protected by a substantial margin of profit'. The range referred to was probably the company's 'Cheap' Bear, a range Farnell described as cheap in price alone. In a catalogue dated a couple of years after the range had been introduced, they explained that the Cheap Bear was a 'line we are frequently asked for to meet foreign competition'. Made from lower-quality mohair than was usual for Farnell bears, it was available in four different sizes – 11, 13.75, 15 and 16 inches – and was sold by the dozen. The smallest size cost thirty shillings per dozen (two shillings and sixpence per bear) and the largest fifty-four shillings per dozen (four shillings and sixpence each). This compares favourably with the Magnet, another cheap mohair bear, introduced by new company Merrythought in 1930; the smallest teddy in the Magnet range cost forty-two shillings per dozen (three shillings and sixpence per bear), a shilling more than the 'Cheap' Farnell. Admittedly the smallest Cheap Bear was 1.5 inches smaller than the smallest Magnet but even the next size up in the

This large and handsome bear dates from the
1930s; made from short, thick golden mohair,
it may have been part of the Teddy Series.

Large Farnell teddy from the 1930s with super
quality mohair.

Cheap range – which at 13.75 inches was 1.25 inches bigger than the smallest Magnet – cost a few pence less. Clearly Farnell were following a very deliberate policy of undercutting their rivals in the budget market.

Another new line introduced around the same time as the Cheap Bear was the Teddy Series, a high-quality bear made in what Farnell described as a highly improved plush. Where the Cheap Bear was unashamedly targeted at the bottom end of the market, the Teddy was a fine-quality bear which the company was able to offer at a competitive price thanks to its turnover and purchasing power. It was available in nine different size options – 12.5, 14, 15, 16.5, 18.5, 20.5, 21.5, 24 and 26.5 inches – and for some of these sizes Teddy could be supplied in art silk plush or white mohair plush. The wholesale price for the largest, the 26.5-inch bear, was seventeen shillings and sixpence but by the time a retailer had sold it to a member of the public, it probably cost at least twice that amount. This was a substantial sum to spend on a toy considering the average wage for a clerical worker around this time was four pounds and fifteen shillings. Small wonder, then, that Farnell had felt the need to produce the Cheap Bear as a less costly alternative.

Even so, the Teddy was not the most expensive Farnell teddy bear on the market in the 1930s. In fact, it was only the firm's mid-price teddy bear, the honours for being the most costly falling to the Alpha Bear, which was reintroduced in 1935 just as the worst effects of the Wall Street Crash were receding and wages had started to rise. As a growing number of people began to feel more secure in their finances, Farnell decided the time was right to bring back the Alpha Bear, the teddy-shaped jewel in the company's crown, which was acclaimed as the best bear on the market. Made, so its manufacturer boasted, in the finest materials procurable, the Alpha Bear was unequalled for 'quality, finish and appearance'. The unparalleled

Available in three sizes, this soft alpaca teddy came in four colours suitable for the nursery.

BEARS

No.	Per doz.	Height
1	36 –	9½"
2	44 –	10½"
3	48 –	12½"

excellence of the plush Farnell used was a constant theme at this time. 'The plushes used are the finest procurable,' announced *Games and Toys*, 'and Messrs. Farnell acknowledge the assistance and co-operation of one of the greatest plush manufacturers in Yorkshire, who has taken an immense amount of trouble to provide plushes which place the British soft toy pre-eminent.' Thanks to Farnell's buying power, the company was able to reserve some of this premier plush for its exclusive use.

The 1935 catalogue offered the Alpha Bear in no fewer than eleven different size options – 9.75, 11.25, 12.5, 14.25, 15.75, 17.75, 20.25, 21.75, 23, 26.5 and 29.5 inches. This last size represented a fairly serious financial investment since its wholesale price alone was twenty-seven shillings and sixpence. Nevertheless, the company must been confident that the return of the Alpha Bear would please customers and certainly the trade press was delighted to welcome back toys which were 'the very acme of quality', in the words of *Games and Toys*.

Teddy variations – Captain Bruin, Podgie, Bobbles etc

While the Alpha, Teddy and Cheap Bear covered all bases in the market for traditional teddy bears, a sizeable number of less traditional ursine creations appeared in Farnell's portfolio in the mid-to-late 1930s. Some of them came and went without making much of an impact while others were successful in their day but are not remembered today because they have not survived in significant quantities. It is not possible to supply an exhaustive list of these bear variations because Farnell's records appear to have been lost. All the same, quite a few can be identified thanks to a combination of entries in a rare catalogue estimated to date from 1935, contemporary references in the trade press and actual examples of labelled bears which date from that time. For example, a clown bear dating from

Made of artificial silk plush, Captain Bruin is rarely found today.

"CAPTAIN BRUIN"

Alpha bears of the 1930s came in 11 different sizes; at around 12.5 inches, this example is one of the smallest.

A larger Alpha Farnell bear made from shaggy, light brown tipped mohair.

the 1930s turned up at auction a few years ago. Measuring around 15 inches, it was made from orange artificial silk plush and was wearing an orange felt ruff. It may at one time have had a clown hat and the same design was almost certainly offered in different colours. Then, thanks to the 1935 catalogue, we know that an appealing jointed teddy with a sweet face was produced as part of what seems to have been a nursery range that also included four different rabbits, a standing dog and a polar bear cub in a 'sit up and beg' position. The jointed teddy was made from very soft alpaca in three different sizes – 9.5, 10.75 and 12.5 inches – and it had short-ish arms, chunky thighs and sturdy legs. Colour options were white, coral pink, soft blue and gold. As for price, it was positioned a little ahead of the rock-bottom Cheap Bear, with the smallest size costing 36 shillings per dozen, wholesale. The begging polar bear was also available in three sizes – 6.25, 7.25 and 8.25 inches – and was slightly less expensive at just 24 shillings per dozen for the 6.25 inch piece.

Costumed soft toy animals were popular in the 1930s and as ever Farnell were at the forefront of the trend. In 1935 the company introduced some special novelty lines, which included The Longshoreman (a dressed monkey), Lady Kitty (a cat dressed in a taffeta coat and wearing a poke bonnet) and most importantly of all for bear lovers, Captain Bruin. This fine, quasi-military character measured 12.5 inches high and had white face and legs with an integral tunic made from artificial silk plush in a pastel shade. As no specific shade is mentioned, it seems likely that a variety of colours were available. The use of artificial silk plush increased the cost of Captain Bruin so he was priced at eighty shillings per dozen wholesale, eight shillings more than the same quantity of 16.5-inch traditional bears from the mid-price Teddy Series. Whether or not the design was a commercial success is impossible to know, but it almost certainly caught the eye of one of Farnell's competitors because a couple of years after Captain Bruin had made his debut in the Farnell catalogue a similar-looking bear called Bombardier Bruin appeared in the Merrythought range.

In 1928, Farnell had made waves in the toy trade by introducing a soft toy that could also be used as a nightdress case. The idea seems straightforward enough today but at the time it was regarded as little short of revolutionary. Their first nightdress cases had been intended for use by sophisticated ladies and had carried a high price tag. Two years later, the success of the ladies' nightdress cases had prompted the company to launch their Kiddie Cuddle Nightie Cases, aimed squarely, as the name implies, at the child market. If, as *Games and Toys* suggested, some toy buyers felt that the range stepped outside the proper realm of toys, they soon had to revise this opinion when the nightie cases proved to be a runaway success. Those first child-targeted cases had featured dogs and cats but in the mid-1930s, when teddy bears were making a triumphant comeback, a jolly bear version was introduced. Part of Farnell's range of Podgie Cases that also included Podgie Doll and Podgie Piggie, Podgie Bear was a 20-inch rotund teddy with a compartment in his back for storing night attire and a pocket for a small handkerchief. Lined with silk taffeta, the compartment was opened and closed by a lightning fastener (a type of zip). Although Podgie Bear was

Designed to appeal to younger children, Bobbles was made from dark brown and biscuit-coloured wool plush.

"BOBBLES"

Podgie Bear was part of a range of nightie cases that also included Podgie Pig and Podgie Doll.

"PODGIE" BEAR

intended to be a bedtime toy, he could be supplied with a waterproof lining in his compartment for holding a wet bathing suit, thus making him and his Podgie pals the perfect seaside companions. Of the three varieties – pig, doll and bear – Podgie Bear was by far the most expensive, costing 108 shillings per dozen (wholesale) while Podgie Pig and Podgie Doll were 84 shillings and 54 shillings per dozen respectively. Proud of their new design and anxious to deter copying, Farnell went to the trouble of patenting and registering the Podgie designs.

Another teddy character created by Farnell with younger children in mind was Bobbles, a delightful bear who made his debut in the middle of the decade. Available in four different sizes – 11, 13.5, 14 and 16.5 inches – Bobbles was made from two-tone wool plush with his head and body a dark brown colour and his arms, legs, muzzle, inner ears and two fluffy pom-poms on his front in a contrasting biscuit shade. An unjointed bear, he was stuffed with kapok to make him soft and huggable, and he was finished with a smart ribbon bow tied around his neck. Bobbles had bags of child appeal and since wool plush was less expensive than mohair or artificial silk he was competitively priced (forty-eight shillings per dozen for the largest size, for example). Just like Captain Bruin and Podgie, he is rarely seen today, perhaps because parents tended to throw this type of toy away once they became dirty or worn.

Che-Kee, Alpac, Coronation and more

A quirky little bear produced by Farnell in the middle of the decade is at the centre of a conundrum concerning the material from which it was made. During the 1930s, the firm turned out bears made from mohair, artificial silk, wool plush and alpaca, all of which were fairly standard materials for the era. In 1935, however, the company introduced a new line of toys called the Che-Kee Series, which were made from what they called 'natural skin'. In the range was a 'tree bear', the name Farnell for some obscure reason decided to give to the koala. While the term 'natural skin' could reasonably be expected to refer to animal skins, in the past a number of respected teddy bear authorities have stated that Che-Kee toys were made from lambs' wool plush. Furthermore, a news snippet in the August 1935 issue of *Games and Toys* describes the Che-Kee Series as washable, a believable claim for toys made of wool plush but surely less so for those made of animal skin. On the other hand, although admittedly blurry the Che-Kee items depicted in Farnell's 1935 catalogue do not particularly look as if they have been made from lambs' wool plush. Also, the cost of the 11.5-inch 'tree bear' was 108 shillings per dozen, a lot more than the 48 shillings per dozen charged for the 16.5-inch, wool plush Bobbles. Finally, it is known that when Merrythought created their own koalas in the 1950s the toys were made from what they called 'real Australian skin' and this turned out to be kangaroo skin. Were it not for the 'washable' reference, the evidence would seem to point to skin rather than lambs' wool plush, but since the washable reference cannot be ignored, the matter must remain undecided for the time being. At least the survival of the relevant catalogue page means individuals can study the images and reach their own conclusions. In any case, the 'soft and cuddlesome' Che-Kee toys proved very popular and remained in the Farnell range at least until 1939.

It is unclear whether the toys in the Che-Kee range were made from lambs' wool plush or animal skin.

THE "CHE-KEE" SERIES OF NATURAL SKIN ANIMALS

"CHE-KEE" LONG HAIRED DOG
Natural Skin.   In Silver-Grey or Beige.
Standing Model No. 1100
Sitting   „   „   1110   } 144 – per doz.

"CHE-KEE" PEKINGESE
A most lifelike Model in very long Pure White Natural Skin.
27 6 each.   Length 14"

"CHE-KEE" MONKEY
In long Pure White Natural Skin—Mask with glass eyes.

No.	Each	Height
1	27 6	21
2	40 –	26

"CHE-KEE" SQUIRREL
In Natural Skin. Large bushy tail.
108 – per doz.   Height 12"

"CHE-KEE" TREE BEAR
In Natural Skin.
108 – per doz.   Height 11½"

Top Left: An 8-inch teddy bear from the Alpac range.

Above: Red, white and blue artificial silk Dutch-style teddy, made in 1937, the year of George VI's coronation.

Left: White wool plush bear, 12 inches, dating from the 1930s.

Thankfully, there is no such confusion about a new range introduced by Farnell in 1937. Created especially for babies and young children, the toys in the 'Alpac' series were made from alpaca plush, a very soft textile that is wonderful to touch, and came in a variety of colours. Teddy bears featured heavily in the series, which was described as 'real quality … comprising first-class value'. Dressed teddy bears also appeared in 1937, as did other bears made from mohair, artificial silk, alpaca and wool plush, all of which were sold under the Alpha Toys label. This was the year of King George VI's coronation and Farnell produced a number of superb pieces to mark the occasion, including jointed and unjointed bears in red, white and blue best-quality artificial silk plush. One of the unjointed bears was a 'Dutch-style' teddy, so-called because of its wide legs that were said to resemble the trousers worn in traditional Dutch costume. It was a style of bear manufactured by other companies at the time, although the Farnell version is dissimilar to most others in that it was made from artificial silk plush rather than mohair or alpaca. Measuring about 10 inches high, the bear is unjointed except at the head, and its glass eyes are a striking bright blue colour. The head and paws are of white artificial silk, the chest and 'arms' are a deep red that has darkened almost to maroon over the years, and the hips and legs are midnight blue. A small white tail sticks out of the bear's 'trousers', and there is a narrow white rectangular label on its left foot on which the words 'Farnell's Alpha Toys Made in England' are embroidered in blue. Its kapok stuffing makes the bear very soft, as befits a toy Farnell described as a 'cuddley [sic] bear'.

Throughout the 1930s dolls had been playing an increasingly important role in Farnell's fortunes (see Chapter 7), but even so, the company remained committed to teddy bears. Underlining this point, in an article published in *Games and Toys* in June 1939, Albert E B Rose – Farnell's Managing Director – described the teddy bear as 'the most popular soft toy extant'. Small wonder, then, that the company continued to produce teddy bears in a number of styles and sizes. In 1939 a wide range of bears in sitting, lying and standing positions were offered for the young children's market, and the year also saw the arrival of a new Alpha novelty, the mohair Chubby Bear, who came complete with his own cup and spoon. That old favourite the Alpha Bear was also available in a number of sizes. It was described as 'a high quality line made in a fine plush' and even though its prices were deemed 'attractive' – a euphemism for affordable –

Farnell grasped that they might not be attractive enough to enable everyone to afford an Alpha Bear. Therefore, a less costly range of bears called the 'Sammy' was introduced at a price that made them comparable to cheap foreign imports.

Music, maestro!

In an increasingly competitive market, it was important to find new ways in which to stay ahead of the pack. In 1937, in a bid to do just that, Farnell secured an arrangement with a Swiss music box company, Thorens, which manufactured an innovative product called the 'Thorens Stop and Go Musical Movement'. Toys fitted with the movement would start playing 'a merry tune' when picked up and the tune would stop immediately when the toy was put down again. Recognising the movement's enormous potential in the toy market, Farnell obtained exclusive rights to use the Thorens Stop and Go movement in their soft toys and dolls. There were a number of 'merry tunes' in Farnell's repertoire, including nursery favourites such as 'Hush a Bye, Baby' and 'Three Blind Mice' and even a patriotic number like 'Here's a Health unto His Majesty'. According to contemporary accounts in the trade press, the Stop and Go lines met with considerable success, although it is doubtful whether the 'Chamberlain' Peacemaker doll which played 'For He's a Jolly Good Fellow' was popular once war with Germany broke out in September 1939.

Royal visits

During the 1930s it became customary for members of the royal family to show support for British industry by attending various trade shows. At one such show in 1937, the Farnell stand was graced by a visit from several high-ranking royals. The main attraction for them was undoubtedly the new line of dolls depicting King George VI in various military uniforms but no doubt the eminent visitors also enjoyed looking at the beautiful teddy bears and soft toys. Indeed, it was reported that Queen Elizabeth (wife of George VI) and other members of the party made purchases at the stand, although sadly no mention was made of the items that caught the royal fancy. Teddy bears are a possibility – in one photograph published in *Games and Toys*, the Queen is seen standing admiring a large, bonnet-wearing doll and immediately behind her are shelves lined with teddy bears. A second photo shows Queen Mary (mother of George VI) and her fourth son, the Duke of Kent, inspecting the regal dolls, which were marketed as the Coronation Set. The coronation of George VI took place soon after the photos were taken, in May 1937. He had assumed the throne following the abdication the previous December of his older brother, Edward VIII, who refused to give up the woman he loved, the twice-divorced Wallis Simpson.

Chapter 6

Everything Must Change

(1940–1970)

Having weathered the difficult economic conditions of the 1930s and survived the potentially catastrophic impact of the 1934 factory fire, J K Farnell & Co Ltd was to face plenty of new challenges in the next decade and beyond. This time, however, the company had to manage without the support – practical or moral – of founder Joseph Kirby Farnell's last surviving offspring because both were to die in the first years of the 1940s. Martha Monement was the first to go; her long and somewhat blighted life was ended by a brain haemorrhage on 20 January 1941 and she was laid to rest beside her sisters in the family plot at North Acton Cemetery. London at the time was experiencing the nightly terror of bombing raids in which many civilians, young and old, were losing their lives, so the passing of one elderly lady probably attracted little comment. In her eighty-fifth year at the time of her death, an age none of her sisters had attained, Martha herself may have felt she had little to live for following the death of her only child eleven years earlier.

With Martha gone, Henry was left alone at The Elms with just the toy factory to hold his interest in life. We know for certain that he was still taking an active part in the business as late as 1935 when he was aged eighty-one, and he remained a major shareholder right up until his death. He may also have had his garden to occupy his thoughts – at one time he had been a keen amateur gardener, winning first prize for his delphiniums at the Royal Horticultural Society show in Westminster in 1925 – but at his advanced age, even with assistance gardening was probably now beyond him. With his siblings all gone, the big house must have felt very empty, and although his niece Mary Williams lived in nearby Ealing (Beatrice was in West Sussex) he must have found it hard to resist a downward spiral into loneliness. Sadly, having endured the worst of the war years, he died in 1944, just one year too soon to see the jubilant victory celebrations in London. Henry Kirby Farnell was also buried in the family grave at North Acton Cemetery although his name was never added to the grave's inscriptions; Eleanor, Agnes and Martha are there, their names and dates of death inscribed on three sides of the rectangular plot, but the fourth side remains unmarked. All the same, cemetery records prove that Henry Kirby is definitely there, lying beside the three sisters who shared so much of his life. (Although the grave itself is kept neat by the authorities, the headstone has fallen and now lies flat on top of the grave.)

Following the death of Henry Kirby, no one with the Farnell surname remained at J K Farnell & Co Ltd, but all the same the company was still very much a family business. Mary Williams and Beatrice Hollins remained on the Board of Directors, and when Albert E B Rose resigned from the board in December 1944, his place was taken by Dr Richard Williams, Mary's husband. Rose's resignation so soon after the death of Henry Kirby suggests the two men may have been close. Rose had, after all, been intimately associated with the Farnells ever since his marriage to Frances Monement in 1909 and even after her death and his subsequent remarriage he had remained on good terms with the family. There is evidence to suggest that he had been trying to leave the company for some time – in 1940 he had resigned but had evidently been persuaded to return – and after Henry Kirby's death it may have seemed like the right time to move on. Nevertheless, he remained a shareholder right up until his death in 1966.

War and peace

Due to an absence of records it is not possible to know precisely how Farnell passed the years of the Second World War (1939–1945) but almost certainly at some point the factory would have been given over to vital war work. Toy production probably continued more or less as normal during the early months of the war – the period known to history as the Phoney War – even though important European markets were now closed due to the spreading conflict. Gradually, though, the younger members of the workforce would have left in order to go and help the war effort and the imposition of a ban in 1942 on the production of toys containing kapok would have brought the company virtually to a halt. Even before then, however, the likelihood is that Farnell had been ordered by the government to switch from toy making to manufacturing vital war materials. There is a suggestion that this work involved making airmen's flying jackets and helmets because just after the war quantities of these items were picked apart for use in the manufacture of Farnell teddy bears.

It has been alleged that following Farnell's fire in 1934 the factory was destroyed for a second time, this time by a Luftwaffe bomb in 1940. Finding conclusive confirmatory evidence of this event has proved surprisingly difficult. While Acton was indeed a target for heavy bombing during the Blitz owing to the presence of several important engineering factories, the Alpha Works are not referred to by name in the RAF's daily reports, which recorded the factories, railways lines and other places hit by the enemy bombs (www.raf.mod.uk/Bob1940/bobhome.html). Furthermore, local people to whom I spoke about the war years do not have any recollection of Farnell being damaged or destroyed by a bomb. Stan Hancock, who was born in 1941, was very familiar with bomb-damaged buildings, having played on bomb sites around his home area of South Acton. Stan's mother worked at the Farnell factory and he recalls visiting it in 1946 or 1947. In his recollection there were no obvious signs of bomb damage such as scorch marks or flattened buildings. Similarly Michael Fisher, whose parents had lived in Acton since 1932 and who was himself born there in 1946, had never heard of Farnell being bombed during the war (although he admits that even though he lived just one and a quarter miles from The Elms, because the house was set back and hidden from the road it was years before he knew that it existed and even longer before he discovered that a toy factory had once been there). However, a brief news item from the *Acton Gazette* of 27 September 1940 comes very close to confirming the story. According to this report, early in the morning of Wednesday, 25 September, an incendiary bomb struck a soft toy factory located in an unnamed West London suburb. The flames were visible from all the neighbouring boroughs and the building was left a blackened shell. Although the factory and the suburb in which it was located are unnamed in the report – presumably for reasons of national security – a strong clue is given at the end of the item when the reporter states, 'It is the second time that this factory has been destroyed by fire.' Unlikely as it seems, it is technically possible that another, unknown West London soft toy factory was the subject of the report and therefore it cannot be said to prove the point beyond doubt. However, it is very probable that the factory in question was Farnell and in the absence of evidence to the contradictory, I am inclined to accept it as fact.

On the face of it, the fire would have been another devastating blow for the Farnell family, but happily there was no loss of life as the only victims of the blaze were, to quote from the *Acton Gazette*, 'teddy bears and other woolly animals'. Furthermore, although the story ran under the header 'Raiders Demolish Soft Toy Factory' this is probably a case of journalistic hyperbole because the report mentions the destruction of just one building and, as has been seen, the Alpha Works comprised several buildings. Therefore, bad as the damage inflicted by the incendiary bomb undoubtedly was, it was probably not as completely devastating as initial reading of the report suggests. This would have been just as well for Farnell since I believe there is a strong possibility that later that same year the firm's City showroom was destroyed by a bomb. The showroom was located in New Union Street in the heart of Moorgate, an area that suffered some of the heaviest bombing of the Blitz. According to the Museum of London, on one night alone – 29 December 1940 – almost every building in the Barbican and Moorgate area was destroyed. A photograph taken by a police officer on the morning of 30 December shows New Union Street reduced to rubble and ashes. It is hard to see how the Farnell showroom could have survived such devastation. This theory is supported by entries in contemporary London phone directories. Throughout the 1930s, the entries show the address and telephone number of the Alpha Works in Acton and also of the showroom at New Union Street, EC2; the showroom is still listed in the 1940 directory but it is absent in the following year's directory, although the Acton listing is still there. Not until 1956 does a listing in the telephone book again appear for Farnell's City showroom and when it does the address has changed to Condor House, St Paul's Churchyard, EC4. (An advertisement in the June 1954 edition of *Games and Toys* shows an address in Old Change, Cheapside for Farnell's City showroom; this was probably a stop-gap arrangement until more suitable, permanent premises could be found.) I therefore believe there is a distinct possibility that the New Union Street showroom was utterly destroyed during the raids of 1940–1941 and permanent new premises were not found until the middle of the 1950s.

After the Second World War, things were never quite the same at Farnell. The war had claimed the lives of millions all over the world and altered forever the lives of millions more. When the hostilities had ended, Britain, although technically victorious, was found to be in a terrible condition, struggling to rebuild bomb-flattened cities whilst staving off the threat of total economic collapse. A few unrelentingly hard years were to pass before the country gradually began to recover and when people finally had the opportunity to raise their heads from their labours and take a good look around, many discovered a country they no longer recognised. The attitudes and mores of pre-war society were vanishing, the Empire was crumbling and everyone except the die-hard traditionalists craved modernity in every aspect of their lives – housing, design, music, clothing, even in business. In such an environment, a company like J K Farnell & Co Ltd, founded in Victorian times and perhaps too firmly rooted in its glorious past, was always going to have a tough time adjusting. Practical considerations also had an effect on the company's fortunes. Since the toy making business had virtually been in abeyance during the war years, the order book would have been empty and even if there had been orders the company may not initially have had the materials and manpower to fulfil them.

Margaret Florence Hancock (née Day), more normally referred to as Flo or Florrie, had joined Farnell in 1939 and immediately after the war she worked for them from home. Her son Stan recalls flying jackets and helmets being brought to the house and Flo picking them apart to be recycled in teddy bear manufacture. The leather outers were used for paw pads while the fleecy lining was used for stuffing – materials were in very short supply at the time and everywhere people were obliged to improvise in order to maintain a semblance of normality. As conditions gradually improved, Farnell attempted to carry on much as it had before the war intervened, but too much had changed for that to be possible. A new, leaner operation was called for, producing a reduced number of toys in modern styles that managed to make the most economical use of the available materials while at the same time satisfying the public's desire for novelty.

Although the circumstances were far from ideal, Farnell did manage to make some excellent teddy bears in the 1940s. Due to a lack of the conventional materials, certain of the bears have an atypical appearance, but that only adds to their charm. Some, for example, were made from a lilac-coloured sheepskin, with paw pads made of leather, while others were created from a brown mohair and wool plush combination with rust-coloured felt pads. Other pads could be cloth, painted cloth or rexine. When bears were made from mohair, it was not always in the typical golden or pale golden shades – examples dating from this period have been found made from brown and red–gold mohair. As for facial features, orange or amber and black glass eyes were the norm, and noses, mouths and claws were stitched in black thread. At this stage, the shape of the bears was still similar to pre-war designs, some having elongated, shaped limbs and very slight humps on their backs. These features were to disappear in the 1950s.

Life on the factory floor

The 1950s are fairly barren as far as Farnell catalogues or trade press reports are concerned and without these documents it is hard to be specific about products produced during the decade. Luckily, anecdotal evidence survives in the recollections of people who worked for the company. Having started with Farnell before the war, Flo Hancock stayed until the firm moved to Hastings in the early 1960s. She died in 1996 but her children, Maggie Cue and Stan Hancock, have strong memories of her time with the company. Born in 1908, Flo was one of four or five workers responsible for marking out teddy and toy patterns on to the plush. This involved dipping the pattern pieces into black dye and then putting them on the plush to mark it. When the dye was dry, Flo cut around it. 'I remember her standing for many hours with her hands coated with black paint and very carefully making sure she got as many pieces of teddy out of a piece of plush as she could,' her daughter Maggie remembers. Great rolls of the expensive plush were kept in a storeroom at The Elms while the cutting took place at the Uxbridge Road facility, a very short distance from the house, situated to the right and slightly set back from it. Sometimes Maggie visited her mother's workplace. She would sit in the room where the staff hung their coats, close to where the plush that was soon to be marked was kept. Her mother stood at the end of this area, marking out the bears. The smell of the plush is indelibly stamped on Maggie's memory. 'It was wonderful,' she recalls, 'the smell of my childhood, the smell of teddy bears.' Even today, whenever Maggie is in a shop selling teddies the smell is able to evoke very powerful memories. Regrettably, although she owned a Farnell teddy bear as a child, she no longer possesses it because her father, a generous man, gave the toy away when he thought she no longer needed it. Another of Maggie's memories comes from when she went into one of the grand rooms inside The Elms and looked up at its spectacular painted ceiling. Executed by Francesco Sleter around 1735, the painting depicts the Judgement of Paris, a famous scene from Greek mythology. It was removed from The Elms in the 1950s by Middlesex County Council who subsequently gave it to Gunnersbury Park Museum.

According to her children, Flo Hancock was very proud of the teddy bears made by Farnell, often stating that 'they only go to the good shops like Harrods'. As had been the case before the war, Farnell looked after their employees and as a result there was a low staff turnover. Annual outings to seaside towns and jolly Christmas parties encouraged loyalty and helped foster camaraderie amongst the workers. When they were older Maggie and Stan were also employed by Farnell for a time. Maggie worked there in the school holidays but Stan started his working life with the company in 1957 at the age of fifteen. He was employed as a 'general body' performing various functions as required. At times he turned the cotter pins that joined the teddies' arms to their bodies, at other others he swept floors or took deliveries of kapok and wood wool off vans which arrived from the north of England. He would then take the new deliveries into the 'shed' in the Uxbridge Road for the stuffers to use. At that time the company was being run by Mr W E Hunt and his wife, a very smart couple in their late forties or early fifties. 'Mr Hunt was the boss,' Stan recalls, 'and his wife assisted him.' Mr Hunt – he was always 'Mr Hunt', there was no undue familiarity – was a very polite, dapper man of medium height and build. His wife was dark haired and always very well turned out. 'She looked very professional, always wore a suit,' Stan remembers. Mr Hunt went out and about in a Hillman Minx, which was driven and looked after by Paddy, one of two part-time firemen employed by the company. The second, Charlie, tightened the cotter pin joints, a job that requires a certain amount of wrist strength. Other personnel included William Shackleton who was the Company Secretary and a director, the General Manager Tom King who was also involved in design, and Ted Elliott, the pattern maker. From the pre-war glory days of five or six hundred employees, the workforce in 1957 was now reduced to no more than thirty. This left plenty of empty space in the factory so Farnell sensibly arranged to share some of it with another local company, CAV Ltd, a very large engineering firm which already occupied large premises in Warple Way, Acton. An adjoining wall split the two organisations and they remained entirely separate from one another.

Teds of the 1950s

Although Farnell could no longer be regarded as a big company, it was still a successful one with a continuing reputation for producing high-quality teddies and toys. In Stan Hancock's time, for example, the firm held an important contract with Marks and Spencer. Some of the teddy bears were labelled Alpha

This handsome bear is known to date from the 1940s as he was given to his original
owner as a christening present in 1948.

Immediately after the Second World War, Farnell made teddy bears from whatever materials were available, in this case pink alpaca (the smaller bear dates from the 1960s).

but others had the M&S 'St Michael' label put on, with nothing to identify them as Farnell products. Stan was only aware of teddy bears being made in three sizes, small, medium and large, all of which were made from golden plush. However, reduced as Farnell's productivity undoubtedly was, there was far greater variety than this in the company's output during the 1950s. Perhaps the most prevalent teddy bears of the decade were those made of golden mohair; created in a variety of sizes including 12.5, 14 and 21 inches, they tended to have orange and black glass eyes (although some have been found with plastic eyes), pronounced clipped muzzles and rexine pads. Musical versions of these golden mohair teddies were popular, with a mechanism fitted inside the bear which played a tune when a key was wound. Sometimes golden wool plush or a wool–mohair mix was used as an alternative to mohair, and painted cloth pads might be used instead of rexine. While pronounced clipped muzzles were a feature of many Farnell teddies, a squarer, stubbier muzzle was also sometimes used. Noses and mouths were stitched in black thread, as were any claw stitches. Although less common than the golden colour, white mohair was also used for teddies in the 1950s, usually in conjunction with red felt paw pads. For very young children, there were unjointed bears created from blue, pink and yellow synthetic plush, and also pink and white unjointed teddies made in a seated position, with chime mechanisms that made them ideal nursery toys. These models were probably also available in blue and white, and possibly even yellow and white. In addition to the teddies, a wheeled bear, a descendant of the Anima, was still in production, as were some nightdress cases modelled as bears, and black and white pandas were also being produced. Teddy bears usually had labels attached to a side or chest seam.

Even though the Farnell Stan Hancock worked for was much smaller than the 1930s operation, surprisingly little about the way in which the toys were manufactured had changed. The factory, or 'shed' as Stan refers to it, was still divided into several different areas of activity. At the top section were the markers and cutters; the machinists who sewed the pieces together were next to them with the stuffing department in the adjacent bay. Then came the finishing department where eyes were inserted and mouths and noses stitched on. At the bottom end of the shed was the despatch department where the bears and animals were boxed up and sent out. Mr and Mrs Hunt's offices were also at this end and there was a side section where Mr King and Mr Elliott worked. After working at Farnell for nine months, Stan left to start a career in butchery, but his mother remained until the company completed its relocation to Hastings in the early 1960s.

A new chapter

Following the death of Henry Kirby Farnell in 1944, The Elms remained empty for several years and as a result it had become sadly neglected by the start of the new decade. Inside the house there was widespread damp and dry rot, while outside overgrown foliage now obscured the front of the elegant property. Something had to be done and so in 1953 it was taken over by Middlesex County Council who restored the worst damage and converted it into an extension to Acton Central School. Local craftsmen were called in to reverse the ravages wrought by neglect. A new roof was put on, the woodwork of the extravagant staircase in the grand entrance hall was tenderly restored, dry rot was burnt off

Farnell staff outing, circa 1940s/1950s; Flo Hancock is on the far left, second row down.

Christmas party in the Farnell finishing room; Mr Hunt and Mr Shackleton stand on the left at the back, Flo Hancock sits front row, fourth from the right and across from her is pattern maker Ted Elliott.

At this jolly staff party, Mr Hunt is receiving a gift from staff in fancy dress.

1950s Farnell outing; Mr and Mrs Hunt stand on the far right, Company Secretary Mr Shackleton is at the opposite end and General Manager Tom King is in the back row smoking a pipe.

with a paraffin flame thrower and a bonfire was made of the tangled shrubbery that had for years kept the house hidden like Sleeping Beauty's castle. The ballroom – where Francesco Sleter's Judgement of Paris once graced the ceiling – now became an art room while the first floor provided space for a science room, needlework room and three classrooms. If being transformed into a state education establishment was something of a comedown for this fine building, at least it was saved from the bulldozer, unlike plenty of other historic houses that were lost during the demolition-happy 1950s and 1960s. Spiralling renovation costs attracted comment in the local press but for the annexe's new occupants it was money well spent. Writing in the school's magazine in 1953, pupil Nora Asprey of Form IV A described the new extension as a 'beautiful Georgian house most tastefully decorated'. Keenly aware of the house's history, she wrote, 'Now the rooms, formerly occupied by members of a genteel family, are filled with noisy scholars and the hustle and bustle of school life has begun a new chapter in the

Blond Alpha Farnell bear, circa 1950s, measuring 10 inches and with label on chest.

history of The Elms.' The Farnells, the last 'genteel family' to occupy the house, would surely have approved of Nora's words.

The year after Acton Central School started using The Elms as an annexe, work began on the construction of a brand new school complex on land immediately behind the house. By this time it seems that the Farnell Board of Directors had already decided to leave Acton because the *Acton Gazette* and *West London Post* reported that 'when J K Farnell's toy works' lease comes to an end, there will be another new building on the site and Acton Central School will be merged into a five-form secondary modern school.' The Elms Secondary School duly opened in 1957 while Farnell was still occupying the adjacent factory premises; when the company completed its relocation from Acton in 1964 the factory was taken over by the school and used as an examination centre and a sixth form common room as well as an area for games on wet days. Towards the end of the decade it was finally knocked down and replaced by a series of Nissen-style huts, which were used by the maths department. In the late 1980s these huts were removed to make room for a new sports hall. The final transformation took place in 1981 when The

A modern school building and sports facility stand on the site of the old Alpha Works.

Elms Secondary School morphed into Twyford Church of England High School, so named because of its proximity to Twyford Crescent.

Move to Hastings

As Farnell were not able – or perhaps not willing – to renew their lease on the land occupied by the factory, it became a priority to find new premises. Perhaps because a number of directors and major shareholders lived in the Sussex/Kent region, a decision was made to relocate the factory to this area and in due course suitable premises were found in Hastings on the south coast. On 1 June 1960 the registered office of J K Farnell & Co Ltd changed to Olympia Works, 39 George Street, Hastings, Sussex. Three years later the premises were extended to include 42 George Street, the acquisition funded by a mortgage from Barclays Bank. Not long afterwards the Acton facility closed down and all production moved to Hastings.

It has been stated that a newly formed company called Acton Toycraft then took over the empty Alpha Works, renamed them Twyford Works and began manufacturing soft toys under the trademark 'A Twyford Product'. The men behind this enterprise are said to have been a Mr F W Hase and none other than Mr W E Hunt, the man formerly in charge at J K Farnell & Co Ltd. While there is plenty of physical evidence to prove that teddy bears with a Twyford label were indeed produced, the rest of the story is harder to pin down. As has been seen, far from being occupied by a new company, the Alpha Works were utilised for a time by The Elms Secondary School before being demolished and replaced by huts. Companies House, the government body responsible for incorporating and dissolving limited companies, confirms that Acton Toycraft Ltd traded from 1964–1974 but they are unable to do more than that because all records relating to the company have been destroyed. This means there is no way of checking the company's address or confirming the identity of the directors. There is no mention of Acton Toycraft in the telephone books of the era, and an investigation into the 'A Twyford Product' trademark has drawn similarly unsatisfactory results. There are striking similarities between certain Farnell teddies and those bearing a Twyford label, not altogether surprising considering W E Hunt had worked for Farnell, but it is possible that there may have been an even closer connection between the two companies. Frustratingly, without further investigation it is not possible to know the full story about Twyford bears.

Farnell's white mohair bears often had red felt pads in the 1950s and 1960s.

An 18-inch golden mohair Farnell teddy, circa 1950s.

As for Farnell, at the time of its move to Hastings the company was exporting forty per cent of its output and until the relocation from Acton had been completed the new site dealt exclusively with the overseas orders. Times were rapidly changing, though, and exports were falling off; by 1968 just a quarter of Farnell's products were destined for overseas markets. In fact, within a few years of the move to Hastings, much of the British toy industry would be on the verge of collapse, the victim of rising labour costs, restrictive legislation and, most of all, an influx of cheap imports mainly from the Far East. To British children in the 1960s the words 'Made in Hong Kong' were a very familiar sight on toys. These conditions made survival tough for any UK toy manufacturer but due to their recent move Farnell's circumstances were worse than most. In Acton the company had been able to rely on a skilled, experienced workforce, but in Hastings it was necessary to start from scratch, recruiting and training workers in the art of pattern marking, cutting, assembling, stuffing and finishing. According to some sources the lack of skilled workers led to a decline in quality, the very thing for which Farnell was famed and which kept its products in demand both at home and abroad. People who prized excellence over economy sought out Farnell's teddy bears because the cachet attached to the firm's name told them they were buying a superior product. If that cachet diminished, however, there was no longer any reason to favour Farnell over other manufacturers.

A new line of nursery soft toys, the Mother Goose range, was introduced in 1960. In keeping with the times, these toys were made from nylon, which was washable and was therefore deemed a more suitable material for a child's toy than mohair, which can only be given a gentle surface clean. From a purely aesthetic point of view, nylon teddies were nowhere near as appealing as their classier mohair cousins, and even though many children grew up profoundly attached to their nylon teds traditionalists regarded them as deeply inferior products. Writing about a toy display put on by the British Toy Manufacturers' Association in November 1960, a reporter from *The Times* newspaper regretted that 'the familiar brown teddy bear' had taken a back seat to, amongst other things, a white nylon teddy bear with crimson paws. In time, collective nostalgia for traditional jointed mohair teddy bears was to result in the emergence of limited edition collectors' bears but regrettably the phenomenon of adult teddy bear collectors arrived too late to save Farnell. As the firm's fortunes declined, various attempts were made to increase revenue. One scheme involved an arrangement with Pelham Puppets.

The 1967 company accounts report, 'The commission received through the sale of Pelham Puppets shows an increase of £400 over the previous year's trade.' Sadly, it was not enough to stop the rot and that year Farnell reported a loss of £1,068 (about £13,000 in today's money). It wasn't a vast amount but it may have been enough to cast doubt on the viability of the company's future, in some minds at least. At any rate, four directors resigned in 1967, amongst them the eighty-two-year-old Mary Williams (granddaughter of Joseph Kirby Farnell). In August 1967 Mr Caryl Chilton was appointed the firm's Managing Director, demonstrating that the Farnell tradition of keeping it in the family was still going strong since Mr Chilton's wife, Jane, was the daughter of Beatrice Hollins and thus a great-granddaughter of Joseph Kirby Farnell.

Mr Chilton was doing his best in difficult circumstances to keep the old family firm afloat but it was something of an uphill struggle. In 1968, perhaps in response to requests for a quality mohair bear, he launched a classy new product, the Coney Bear, which was well received by the toy industry. It was selected by the Council of Industrial Design for display at the Design Centre, London and won many orders from American buyers. Made of pure mohair plush, Coney Bears were described in the trade press as 'delightful animals' and 'the offspring of the original teddy bear, of which Farnells [sic] claim to be Britain's pioneers'. The success of the first tranche of Coney Bears led to additions in the range and within a few months they were being offered in four different colours – a 'traditional' honey and three shades of white. An imposing 30-inch version was also introduced, and there was the option to have the Coney Bear in either 'short wool' or 'shaggy-looking, cuddlesome silk mohair'. Two other Farnell bears made at this time were Teddy Terry and Percy Panda; described as 'Farnell specials', nothing is known about them besides their names. By contrast, a famous bear called Toffee – from the 1950s BBC *Listen with Mother* programme – was introduced to the Farnell range in 1960 and is described in detail in Chapter 7.

In 1969, despite the best efforts of Managing Director Caryl Chilton and his fellow directors – Desmond Kirkness, Anthony Lowe, Harry Williams (who had been with the company for almost forty years) and Company Secretary Gordon Daniel – the situation at Farnell was clearly becoming untenable with substantial debts owed to HM Customs and Excise and the Inland Revenue. Therefore in March 1970, in the High Court of Justice, Chancery Division Companies Court, Mr Justice Pennycuick ordered the compulsory winding up of J K Farnell & Co

Ltd. One month later the closure of the company was reported in the *Hastings Chronicle*. Thirty-three workers were made redundant as a result, all women, according to the report. The newspaper did not comment, as it might have, that the UK had just said goodbye to arguably its best and most important teddy bear and soft toy manufacturer. After just over one hundred years, the grand enterprise begun by Joseph Kirby Farnell had finally come to an end. (While the actual closure occurred fairly speedily, the complex winding up procedures moved at a much slower pace. Between 1970 and 1995 no fewer than three Official Receivers were appointed to liquidate the company but in May 1995 it was finally dissolved.)

A family firm to the end

The firm of J K Farnell & Co Ltd began as a family business and despite reports to the contrary remained so to the very end. Of the four directors on the board at the time of the company's winding up, two were married to great-granddaughters of Joseph Kirby Farnell, another was loosely connected to the family by marriage

Trio of unjointed nursery bears in pastel shades of synthetic plush.

Pink and white unjointed bear fitted with a chime movement.

and the fourth may have been a step-relation of some kind. As has been seen, Caryl Chilton was the husband of Beatrice Hollins' middle child, Jane. He was thus a great-grandson-in-law of Joseph Kirby Farnell, as was his fellow board member Anthony Lowe, who was the husband of Beatrice's oldest child, Rosemary. Desmond Kirkness, meanwhile, was married to Anthony Lowe's sister and therefore was brother-in-law to Joseph Kirby Farnell's great-grandson-in-law, a distant family connection to be sure but a connection all the same. Finally, Henry Williams may have been a relative of Dr Richard Williams who married Mary Farnell in 1927 – a son from an earlier marriage, maybe, or else a cousin or nephew. Attempts to establish a relationship have so far failed due to the sheer number of people sharing Henry Williams' name but bearing in mind the company's tendency to keep it in the family there is at least a possibility that he too was in some way connected to the Farnell clan.

Red mohair
Twyford teddy.

The names of the company's final shareholders reveal a similar story. As befitted the sole surviving grandchild of Joseph Kirby Farnell (her sister Beatrice Hollins having died in 1965), Mary Williams held the largest number of shares (2,910) and her husband Richard held a nominal 100. Two of Beatrice's children, Timothy Hollins and Jane Chilton, each held 1,053 shares while their sister Rosemary Lowe held 928, her husband Anthony had 101 and their son Charles had 25. There is irony in the fact that although he was left out of his father's will the descendants of Charles Burcham Farnell ultimately ended up owning the lion's share of the company.

Another major shareholder (and a former director) was a person called Isabel K Rose, who owned 1,235 shares; although she was obviously related to the late Albert E B Rose, her precise identity is hard to establish. She may have been his widow although records give the name of Rose's second wife as Ellen, not Isabel, so she either adopted a different first name or else Rose may have married for a third time. Then again, she may have been his daughter, but since Company House records identify Isabel Rose as a married woman this seems less probable as her surname would have changed from Rose to that of her husband. A third possibility is that she was Rose's daughter-in-law but this again seems far-fetched, particularly as records show she shared a home with Rose until his death in 1966. On balance, it seems most likely that Isabel Rose was Albert E B Rose's widow. She would have inherited the Farnell shares from her husband and he in turn would have inherited them from his first wife, Frances. One other mystery figure, Joan Isobel Sutton, held 895 shares, a substantial amount that suggests she was another Farnell cousin. Finally, Desmond Kirkness, his wife Pauline and Henry Williams held one share a-piece.

Chapter 7

The Other Farnells

Although it is mostly for their fabulous teddy bears that Farnell are remembered today it is important not to overlook the role played in the company's long history by the enormous number of soft toy animals and dolls that they produced. As has been seen, Farnell were making soft toys thirty-five years or so before the teddy bear was invented and even after Teddy had conquered the toy world there were periods when other toy animals, notably dogs, threatened to usurp his throne. Furthermore, Farnell's ability to capitalise on the popularity of animal characters made famous from books, newspapers and so on played a significant part in establishing the firm as the UK's leading soft toy manufacturer.

Getting into character

Today, character merchandising is routine; indeed when it comes to certain sectors of film and television production it sometimes seems as if a character's potential for profitable spin–offs is more important than any other consideration. A hundred years ago, however, the phenomenon of character merchandising was in its infancy and companies like Farnell were at the forefront. The trend was noticed by Beatrix Potter following the publication by Frederick Warne & Co of her third book, *The Tale of Squirrel Nutkin*. The book was published in August 1903 and by Christmas Farnell's versions of the impertinent red squirrel could be found in the London shops. Made of reddish-brown mohair, it had a swivel head, jointed limbs and a wonderfully upright, bushy tail. 'There is a run on toys copied from pictures,' Miss Potter commented, and promptly reacted by copyrighting her own design for a Peter Rabbit toy. (Despite her foresight, ninety years were to pass before a Peter Rabbit 'doll' made from her design materialised, although Steiff versions of Peter Rabbit appeared in 1905.) As far as the history of Farnell is concerned, the significance of their Squirrel Nutkin toy is twofold: it is one of the earliest soft toys that can be positively attributed to the company, and it is their first known venture into character merchandising.

A few years after the production of Farnell's Squirrel Nutkin the firm created a soft toy version of another Beatrix Potter animal. *The Tale of Jemima Puddle-Duck* was published in 1908 and Farnell registered their design for Jemima Puddle-Duck by 1910. In three different size options – 8, 10 and 13 inches – Jemima was made from white mohair and had a swivel head, jointed legs with orange felt feet, an orange beak and black bead eyes made of glass. To match Beatrix Potter's iconic illustrations of the gullible duck, the toy was dressed in a paisley shawl and a blue bonnet. It appeared in the Harrods Christmas catalogue of 1910.

Gone to the dogs

Caesar, another Farnell character toy, appeared in the very same catalogue and remained in production at least until 1926. The real Caesar, a white fox terrier, had been the favourite pet of King Edward VII. The king doted on the little dog, which accompanied him everywhere. In her memoirs Elizabeth, Countess of Fingall describes how Caesar would sneak into her room to share her breakfast whenever she and the king both happened to be staying with Baron and Lady Iveagh at Elveden in Norfolk; having been more than happy to know her as he ate her food, he would ignore her as soon as he was back with his royal master. When Edward died in May 1910 the little dog wandered the corridors of Buckingham Palace, searching disconsolately for the king. A few days later he captured the hearts of the nation when he was seen walking behind the king's coffin during the sombre funeral procession. Such was the little dog's fame that several companies including Steiff and Bing seized on the idea of creating a Caesar toy but Farnell were quick off the mark and their version was on sale in Harrods by Christmas 1910. Measuring 7 inches high and 10.5 inches long, it was made of white mohair with black ears, had orange and black glass eyes, a swivel head, jointed legs and a leather collar.

Caesar was one of the first in a long succession of hugely popular toy dogs created by Farnell. Another was Pip, a mongrel dog character created in 1919 by Bertram Lamb, the editor of the *Daily Mirror*'s children's pages. To begin with Pip had just one companion, a penguin called Squeak, but within a year Lamb had

Games and Toys illustration of Farnell's Pip, Squeak and Wilfred.

introduced a third character, a baby rabbit called Wilfred who spoke just two words: 'gug', a baby word with no specific meaning, and 'nunc', his way of saying 'Uncle' (in reference to Uncle Dick, with whom the trio were said to live). Joined together, the two words formed 'gugnunc', and this was the name used by fans of Pip, Squeak and Wilfred to describe themselves. In 1927 a society called the Wilfredian League of Gugnuncs was formed with the stated aim of making the world a better place. Membership soon reached in excess of 100,000, annual rallies were held at the Royal Albert Hall and special events staged to raise money for good causes. An advertisement in *Games and Toys* confirms that Farnell were creating toy versions of all three characters by February 1922 but by 1925 references to the trio had disappeared from the trade press, which might suggest that they had been dropped from the Farnell range, perhaps because the licence had been awarded elsewhere. A line that lasted much longer was Beauty, a collie pup character that did not require a licence since it was created by Farnell themselves. It was certainly already an established line by February 1922 and remained in production at least until 1935. In February 1926 *Games and Toys* described Beauty as 'one of the biggest selling lines of soft toys in the world'. At the time, Beauty was made in nine different sizes – including a life-size show piece intended for shop window display – and various positions including sitting, standing and begging. A wheeled Anima version was also produced.

The success of Beauty prompted Farnell to devise further dog characters, many of which met with the same level of success enjoyed by the winsome collie pup. In 1925 alone, the public was introduced to Ginger, a comical looking dog of indeterminate breed with 'movable eyes'; Chin-Chin, a Pekinese which reportedly required nine months' design effort before the right colour for the fur could be achieved; Rags, an Irish setter; Sealyham Jim, a white Sealyham terrier; and Scottie, a 'Highland terrier finished in black and made from white chinchilla plush'. Scottie came with a tartan ribbon around his neck and was made in standing and begging positions. Three years later, the company tried a radical new approach to product marketing when it launched Buster, its latest dog character. Described as a cross breed, Buster was clearly some sort of pug. Made in sitting and standing positions, he was produced in sizes ranging from 7.5 to 26 inches (sitting) and 6 to 13 inches (standing) and there was a small 'Baby Buster' which retailed at three shillings and sixpence. In a bold departure from normal practice, Farnell decided to advertise Buster in the *Daily Mail* newspaper. With a daily circulation at the time of five million copies, the paper was able to bring Buster to the attention of exactly the kind of reasonably affluent middle-class consumers Farnell were chasing. The ads appeared in October 1928 in order to drum up

Advertisement from 1926 showing several Farnell bestsellers including Beauty (top row, far right), Ginger (top row, second left) and Dinkie (bottom row, right).

BUY BRITISH

BUY BUSTER

A national advertising campaign made Buster a must-have toy for Christmas 1928.

| MANCHESTER Deansgate Hotel, Jan. 7th—17th. | Mr. T. B. WRIGHT will exhibit a comprehensive collection. |

WRITE FOR OUR ILLUSTRATED CATALOGUE IN COLOUR.

J. K. FARNELL & CO., LTD.

ALPHA WORKS, ACTON HILL, LONDON, W. 3

Telephone—Chiswick 0840.   Telegrams—"Alphatoiz, Act, London."

London Showrooms—19, **NEW UNION STREET, MOORGATE, E.C.2**
Telephone—London Wall 7113.

THE J. K. FARNELL & Co., Ltd. DEPT. of LOUIS WOLF & Co., Inc.
215-219, Fourth Avenue, New York.

SOCIÉTÉ ANONYME J. K. FARNELL, 80, Rue du Faubourg St-Denis, Paris.

Please mention " GAMES AND TOYS " when writing to advertisers.

interest for Christmas and Farnell supported them with a sustained and sophisticated marketing campaign, which included sending colour catalogues and circulars to the toy trade. The campaign was such a resounding success that Buster had achieved worldwide fame within six months. By 1930, for an extra charge Buster could even be fitted with a 'best quality musical box'. Further canine hits came in the guise of Doggie Monty, another unidentified breed with an 'extremely winsome face' and a blue ribbon round his neck, and Doodie, a comical little dog in the begging position, with sideways-glancing eyes and a protruding tongue. Still the public's appetite for Farnell dogs remained unsated and so further characters emerged from the Alpha Works including Angus the Aberdeen, Nibs, Peke Wu, Rex the Sheep-Dog and Cannie the Cairn, to name just a few. When the Unicorn range of cheaper toys was introduced dogs called Spot and Dusty appeared and the latter immediately proved to be a runaway success, so much so that he was relaunched in 1935 as part of the Alpha range. Interestingly,

White mohair
terrier, 7 inches,
circa 1920s/1930s.

it seems that Dusty appealed as much to grown women as to children and he could frequently be found 'in my lady's boudoir', to use the quaint terminology of *Games and Toys*. Made from 'novel mohair plush', which was specially created for Farnell and was not used in the manufacture of any other toy, Dusty was produced in a sitting position with four size options and standing with five size options. The most expensive standing option retailed at seven shillings and sixpence, as did its counterpart in the sitting position.

Chloe Preston and Farnell's velvet mascots

Famous in her day for her charming illustrated children's books, Chloe Preston designed a series of soft toy animals and dolls for Farnell in the 1920s. Born in 1887, her real name was Beatrice Zoe Preston (it is not known when or why she began calling herself Chloe), and she was the only child of a wealthy landowner who owned Moreby Hall, near Bishopthorpe in Yorkshire, and other substantial land holdings. She was educated at home where she developed a talent for art and in 1910, at the age of just twenty-three, her first book was published. Entitled *The Peek-a-Boos*, it featured her own words and illustrations depicting charmingly chubby, round-eyed children. Following the success of the book her family registered the Peek-a-Boos and further books and spin-off toys ensued. At the end of the First World War she moved to Chelsea where she continued to create popular artwork, which was used on postcards, prints and advertising posters. In

1925 she entered into an arrangement with Farnell which resulted in the company creating soft toy versions of several of her designs, including Dinkie the dog (allegedly a Pekinese) and Blinkie the black cat. Made of blue and cream or peach and white velvet, Dinkie measured just over 4 inches high and had brown and black glass googly eyes, which gave him a very droll appearance. His feline companion had similar eyes and was made from black and cream velvet. Both had swivel necks and were stuffed with kapok, 'which is the most expensive stuffing material used in manufacturing' according to *Games and Toys*, to make them soft and cuddly to the touch. By 1926 the public's favourable reaction to Dinkie and Blinkie encouraged Farnell to extend the range and so they were joined by Ginger the comic pup, Ole Misery the hound dog, Bolo the bulldog pup and Toto the mastiff. Interestingly, trade reports did not attribute these later designs to Chloe Preston, but their similarity to Dinkie and Blinkie is unmistakable. Farnell's velvet mascots were *the* craze of 1926 and the firm manufactured no fewer than half a million of them. Preston also designed dolls for Farnell, including examples called Mary, Billie Bimbo and Pal Peter, and in 1927 she created another toy animal, Chinkie, which was predicted to be a winner 'on account of its originality', but alas, no other description was given, so it is not known whether Chinkie was another dog, cat or indeed an entirely different animal species.

Fabulous felines

Prolific as Farnell were in their output of dog toys, they nevertheless found room in their repertoire to accommodate a large and varied selection of other animals. While never coming close to rivalling the canines, many different cats emerged from the Alpha Works over the years, some of which were to prove very memorable. From as early as the First World War years (1914–1918) the company was manufacturing tiny pin-jointed cats made of black mohair. It is widely supposed that these 'lucky black cats', measuring less than 4 inches high, were intended to be presented to loved ones heading off to the war. Although there is no firm evidence to support this supposition, it is a fact that the lucky black cat was a popular theme at the time so the idea seems quite feasible. A soft toy version of a rather different black cat was created by the firm in the early 1920s. In the last years of the silent movie era, Felix the Cat starred in a series of highly popular animated 'shorts'. His screen debut was in 1919 but it wasn't until 1922 that he really took off and then suddenly he was everywhere, his instantly recognisable

THE LATEST NOVELTY IN SOFT TOYS

The popularity of Lady Kitty led to the production of a musical version.

MUSICAL LADY KITTY

black body, saucer-like white eyes and Cheshire Cat-like grin appearing in a comic strip and on a profusion of merchandise, including soft toys. Trade press advertisements and articles confirm Farnell were making their versions of Felix no later than 1925. Created from black mohair with white mohair muzzle, they appear to have been made in a number of different sizes, of which the smallest was about 5.5 inches.

Apart from Felix, Chloe Preston's Blinkie and the lucky black cat, Farnell felines seem to have been few and far between until 1928, when the designers apparently woke up to the fact that many children are as fond of cats as they are of their canine rivals. That year saw the launch of 'the fighting cat', a black tomcat with a tail made of real bushy fur and Kitty, a fluffy Persian kitten available in a choice of white or grey plush. The same unimaginative soul that named the fluffy

Persian Kitty was doubtless also responsible for dubbing a black kitten made from alpaca wool plush Sooty. Yet another Persian kitten, described as 'amusing looking', was called Tiddles and was available in white, grey and black. The following year a 'blue' Persian cat called Kittikins was introduced to great acclaim. Made from a beautiful grey mohair plush, Kittikins made a big impact on the writer from *Games and Toys* when he saw it at the British Industries Fair that year; it was, he decided, 'one of the best toys in the whole of the exhibit'. The public agreed and so Kittikins was back the following year in its original guise and also as a nightdress case, and it was now offered in a tabby-effect mohair as well as the grey used for the 'blue' Persian.

Cats were not much mentioned during the Unicorn years but in 1935, following the factory fire and subsequent reconstruction, Kittikins was back. Two years later it was still in demand and a third colour option, white, was introduced. Also that year, a number of dressed cats put in an appearance, but the real star of 1937 was a musical version of Lady Kitty, a white art silk cat first introduced in 1935. Lady Kitty wore a taffeta coat and a poke bonnet in contrasting shades and measured 14 inches to the brim of her bonnet. Her musical element came via a Thorens Stop and Go musical movement which played a tune when she was picked up and stopped when she was put down. An outstanding success for Farnell, Lady Kitty could, like Kittikins, be purchased as a nightdress case. One other Farnell feline is worth mentioning for its rarity: very occasionally a Farnell Puss in Boots crops up at auction and from its appearance it would seem to date from the 1930s, but the precise date of manufacture is unknown.

Rabbits, elephants and monkeys

Dogs and cats aside, the only other animals to make a significant impact in Farnell's output over the years were rabbits, monkeys and elephants. As has been stated already Wilfred the rabbit was a huge hit in the early 1920s and later in the decade Bunny, a rabbit made of brown and white chinchilla and white plush, put in an appearance. At the same time, brightly coloured rabbits in red, mauve, pink, pale blue, orange and green went on sale. The next rabbit toys of note appeared in 1935, amongst them Nibbles, a crouching rabbit, and dressed rabbits, made in pastel shades of artificial silk plush and wearing blouses and red felt trousers. An especially attractive model this year was the Angora Rabbit, made from a beautifully silky mohair plush in either white or fawn. Available in two sizes – 12

Dating from the early 1920s, this John Willy has aged well, although his thick brown
mohair has acquired a greenish tinge.

and 13 inches long – the Angora Rabbit cost forty-eight shillings and sixty-six shillings per dozen respectively. Two years later, in February 1937, Farnell rabbits enjoyed what was probably their finest hour with a show piece devoted entirely to them. In front of a background scene hand-painted with flowers and trees sat a rabbit dressed as a cobbler, a sign advertising 'Cobling [sic] repairs' beside him. Also in the scene were two mother rabbits, three boy rabbits and one baby rabbit, all attractively dressed. Measuring 60 inches wide and 30 inches high, the scene could be bought for displaying in a shop window. Another bonny bunny from 1937 was a partially dressed character called Happy, so named, perhaps, on account of the large carrot he held.

Monkeys in general were not made in vast quantities by Farnell but two particular designs proved very successful for the firm. The first, Chimpee, was an established line by 1925. Produced in various sizes, he was a jointed toy available in a choice of dark brown, brown and white and white woolly plush. His most distinguishing feature was his open mouth from which his tongue hung out. Chimpee was still popular in 1929 when he was the centrepiece of a delightfully humorous Farnell show piece called Chimpee at School. Dating from the same era and just as popular as Chimpee was a monkey character called John Willy. Like Chimpee, John Willy was made in a variety of colours, but his mouth was firmly closed. His eyes were clear glass with black pupils and his ears, hands, feet and upper face were made of felt. He was fully jointed and stuffed with wood wool, his long tail was wired and his mohair was dense and lustrous. Later Farnell monkeys included the Longshoreman, a monkey dressed in nautical gear, the Che-Kee Monkey, made in long 'pure white natural skin', and Zoo-Zoo, a natural-looking monkey with glass eyes and made from long, biscuit-coloured plush.

While Farnell were prepared to invent their own monkey characters, such as Chimpee and John Willy, when it came to elephants they tended to obtain licences to produce well-known characters from book and film. In 1935, for example, they acquired sole rights to manufacture Babar, Arthur and Celeste, the main characters from the Babar books by Jean de Brunhoff, in the British Isles, British Empire and America. They made charming, dressed versions of all three characters, which occasionally come up for auction at specialist sales although they are not always identified as the Jean de Brunhoff characters. Another elephant character created under licence was Mumfie, the elephant star of Katherine Tozer's popular books. Farnell's Mumfie wore a short coat and shoes and had comically outsized ears. More elephant excitement hit Acton in September 1937 with the announcement that Farnell had reached an exclusive arrangement with London Film, producers of that year's hit film *Elephant Boy*, to create doll versions of Sabu, the eponymous hero, and his elephant.

Dolls

It could be argued that dolls do not belong in a book about teddy bears but it would be a mistake to overlook the contribution their soft dolls made to Farnell's fortunes in the 1930s. In the previous decade a number of dolls had been produced, including some designed by Chloe Preston, and in 1933, at the height of the Unicorn era, a doll called Babs was launched. Manufactured in four different colours – pink, blue, green and orange – Babs had a baby face and her body was made from high-quality wool plush. Elements of Babs were borrowed for the Podgie Dolls nightdress cases which appeared in June 1935 (Podgie Bears were also produced, see Chapter 5). However, it was the arrival of the Alpha Cherubs and the Alpha Joy Day dolls later that year that really established Farnell as leading manufacturers of soft dolls. When the factory premises were rebuilt following the fire of 1934, a new facility devoted entirely to the creation of high-class dolls was included. Retailing at fifteen shillings and eleven pence, Alpha Cherubs were intended to be life-like replicas of real children and they wore clothes similar to contemporary children. Amongst others the series included Tennis Girl, Farm Boy and Village Belle. There were six dolls in the less-expensive Alpha Joy Day range, which retailed at nine shillings and eleven pence each and included Dutch Girl, School Girl and Sailor Boy. A budget range, the Alpha Smilers, was introduced at the same time. There were six Smilers – Airman, Sailor, Sweep, Dutch Boy, Soldier and Page Boy – and they retailed at two shillings and eleven pence a-piece. The masculine characters suggests they may have been intended for small boys, perhaps to pacify them when their sisters were bought the more expensive Joy Day or Cherub dolls.

Games and Toys hailed the new dolls as the embodiment of first-class workmanship, style and finish, and the public agreed, buying them in their thousands. New designs followed, notably in 1937 with a series modelled on the new King, George VI, showing him in his Coronation robes as well as the uniforms of a Grenadier Guard, a Highland regiment and the Royal Air Force. A special 'Coronation Set' of these last three could be purchased for the not-inconsiderable sum of three guineas. The dolls proved to be a real feather in Farnell's cap, garnering lavish praise and a visit to their stand at the British Industries Fair by no lesser personages than Queen Elizabeth (the king's wife), Queen Mary (his mother) and his brother, the Duke of Kent. Other new dolls for 1937 included several 'character studies' including Peter Pan, Pierrot and dolls of different nations, while the Alpha Joy Day range featured some special dolls made with jointed arms and legs. Exquisitely gowned lady dolls dubbed the Alpha 'Sofa' Dolls by Farnell also proved popular in 1937 and were to be found in the boudoirs of many sophisticated women. Two years later, the big story as far as dolls were concerned was the launch of Farnell's Rock-a-Bye Baby dolls, which were made

Royal visit to a Farnell show stand in 1937; Queen Mary is seen admiring the Coronation dolls.

Doll modelled on George VI, showing
him dressed in the uniform of the
Grenadier Guards, circa 1937.

from a new patented process. Described as washable, unbreakable and extremely light, they were supplied both dressed and undressed. Impossibly proud of their new dolls, Farnell succumbed to some uncharacteristically frenzied advertising. 'It is impossible to express in words the super qualities of the "Rock-a-Bye" Baby Dolls,' their advert trumpeted. 'They are so outstanding that only a personal inspection will ever bring home their outstanding superiority of anything yet produced.' Perhaps it was a case of pride coming before a fall because war broke out in September 1939 and afterwards Farnell were never to achieve the same success with dolls. In fact, little is known about their post-war doll output bar the fact that in the 1960s the Mother Goose range of washable nylon toys made in nursery colours was introduced and a number of dolls – including models called Bunny and Pixie – featured in the range.

Alpha Joy Day doll from the mid-1930s.

Time for bed

Invented by Farnell in 1928, the toy animal nightdress case became an immediate bestseller and remained popular to the very end. The first, expensive models were soon followed by cuddly, child-friendly cases that doubled as bed-time toys. Initially ten models including King Charles Spaniel, Peke-Wu, Pom and Kittikins were available and they sold in two price ranges, fourteen shillings and eleven pence and seventeen shillings and sixpence. More complex designs were introduced over time; February 1937, for example, brought a case decorated with two love birds and another with two small dogs in each corner. While novelties like these came and went, the most enduringly popular nightdress case designs were the realistic dog breeds, especially the Pekinese and the terriers. As late in the company's history as 1968, the range of nightdress cases was increased in order to appeal to as wide an age group as possible.

Making a show

From lavishly illustrated colour catalogues to complex and eye-catching displays at trade shows, it is clear that Farnell understood the value of showmanship. Year after year the trade press lauded their catalogues in language that makes it plain such wonders were not the norm. In August 1929, for example, *Games and Toys* wrote:

> Many of our readers will have undoubtedly had a copy of Farnell's catalogue, and we are sure they will agree with us that this production is worthy, not only of Farnell's, but of the British toy trade. As becomes one of the leading soft toy manufacturers in the world, Messrs. J.K. Farnell and Co., Ltd do things in a manner which is worthy of their position, and in issuing their general catalogue for 1929 they have indeed enhanced their already considerable reputation.
>
> The catalogue itself consists of 35 pages and covers. It is profusely illustrated, many of the illustrations being in the actual colours [author's underlining] of the articles themselves. Not alone are they satisfied in issuing this yearly work, but they have recently sent out to their friends in the trade a very handsome supplementary catalogue giving details of their latest productions, the illustrations being in the actual colours of the articles.

K. C. SPANIEL   "PEKE-WU"

"KIDDIE CUDDLE" NIGHTIE CASES

TRADE GENERALLY IS FACED WITH A DIFFICULT YEAR, AND TOY BUYERS WILL FIND IT MORE NECESSARY THAN EVER TO STIMULATE PUBLIC INTEREST BY SOMETHING NOVEL AT A REASONABLE PRICE. WE THINK WE HAVE FOUND THIS IN THE FORM OF A TOY WHICH COMBINES ATTRACTIVENESS, A KIDDIE NIGHTIE CASE, AND A BEDSIDE PET.

"KIDDIE CUDDLE" CASES ARE MADE IN TEN MODELS TO SELL AT 14/11 AND 17/6 EACH.

MR. T. B. WRIGHT WILL BE SHOWING A COMPLETE RANGE OF THIS LATEST IDEA IN TOYS AT THE DEANSGATE HOTEL, MANCHESTER, FROM JUNE 16TH—27TH, OR FULL PARTICULARS MAY BE OBTAINED FROM OUR SHOWROOMS.

J. K. FARNELL & CO. LTD.

Showrooms : 19 NEW UNION ST., MOORGATE, LONDON, E.C.2

Telephone—Metropolitan 7113

"KITTIKINS"   "POM"

Nightdress cases sold under the Kiddie Cuddle brand name were bestsellers for Farnell.

The exhibition stands received no less attention than the catalogues. One of the most memorable was a gypsy encampment assembled at the British Industries Fair in 1939. In front of a painted backdrop were placed a caravan, several gypsy dolls of both sexes, a horse, wooden logs, a campfire and cooking pot. Each doll in the scene could be purchased individually for four shillings and sixpence or the whole display scene could be purchased for the princely sum of ten pounds.

Chapter 8

Favourite Farnells

Within the close-knit community of arctophiles (teddy bear collectors) the significance of J K Farnell & Co Ltd as a pioneering teddy and soft toy manufacturer has long been appreciated, even if the facts have become muddled over time. To the rest of the world, however, the company's claim to fame rests squarely on the shoulders of one toy, a celebrity bear that has spawned a multi-million dollar industry and is famous across the globe. That bear, of course, is A A Milne's Winnie the Pooh.

Farnell's place in the Winnie the Pooh story is at the very beginning. One August day in 1921, an elegant young woman called Daphne Milne went to Harrods in Knightsbridge to buy a teddy bear as a gift for her son, Christopher Robin, who was about to celebrate his first birthday. The bear she chose was one of Farnell's splendid Alpha Bears, about 24 inches high with glorious mohair, light golden in colour, and a rather solemn countenance. The process by which his mother chose the bear was later imagined by Christopher Milne in his autobiography, *The Enchanted Places* (published by Methuen in 1974). He envisaged a row of seemingly identical teddy bears sitting in a toyshop, each one looking slightly different despite their outward similarity. Some might have a stand-offish expression and others would look loveable, but after studying them all, one with 'a specially endearing expression' would have been selected. It is a situation with which many teddy bear collectors can identify because however alike manufactured bears appear to be at first glance close study always reveals a multitude of minute but important differences.

In due course, the boy and his toy bear, initially referred to simply as 'Bear', 'Teddy' or 'Edward Bear', became inseparable companions. Involved in all of Christopher Robin's daytime activities, by night the Alpha Farnell slept inside the nursery ottoman at the Milnes' house in Chelsea. The family spent their weekends and summer holidays at their farmhouse on the edge of the Ashdown Forest in Sussex and whenever they travelled between the two homes the teddy bear always went with them. The origins of the name Winnie the Pooh have been much debated over the years, with various people offering differing explanations. There is nothing unusual in this; many families make up pet names that seem inexplicable to outsiders, having originated perhaps from a chance expression, incident or joke. Over time the names may evolve so much that eventually even the family members themselves scarcely remember how they originated, let alone anyone outside the intimate family circle. This seems to be what happened with Winnie the Pooh, although at least there is a rational explanation for the first part of the name. Winnie was the abbreviated name of Winnipeg, a black bear that Christopher Robin encountered at London Zoo. The bear had been brought to England at the start of the First World War as the unofficial mascot of the Fort Garry Horse, a Canadian cavalry regiment. When the regiment embarked for France in 1915, its vet, Lieutenant Harry Colebourn, left Winnie at London Zoo where she became a popular attraction. Through influential friends, the Milnes were able to arrange for their small son to have a closer encounter with Winnie than was generally available to less well-connected individuals. Understandably

Lieutenant Harry Colebourn with Winnipeg, the bear whose name was borrowed for Winnie the Pooh.

uneasy to begin with, the child hesitated before stepping forward to stroke the bear. Nerves overcome, he decided Winnie was a fine animal and her name was duly appropriated for his toy bear.

So much for Winnie, but how did 'the Pooh' come about? The name Winnie the Pooh is so familiar today that it takes a moment or two of thought to realise how delightfully odd it really is. If the teddy bear Winnie was to become *the* anything, why not Winnie the Bear, or Winnie the Teddy? Legend has it that the name 'Pooh' had originally been given by Christopher Robin to a swan he used to see swimming on a lake in Arundel in Sussex. For some reason – and children usually have their own immutable logic for these things – the swan's name was taken and bestowed as a second name on the bear, with the definite article separating Winnie and Pooh, perhaps because its addition imparted a sense of grandeur. Usually, however, the bear was referred to simply as Pooh. (The word 'pooh' does not appear to have had any unpleasant connotations at the time; when used it was usually to denote nonchalance or bravado as in, 'Pooh! That doesn't bother me one bit!')

So attached was Christopher Robin to his bear that he often used to hold conversations with him, using gruff speech when Pooh was supposed to be talking in order to differentiate it from his own childish voice. Sometimes Pooh was made to say things that the child himself would not be able to say with impunity. According to one story, for example, he came down from the nursery one day while the actor Nigel Playfair was visiting. In his assumed gruff voice he said, 'What a funny man. What a funny red face.' When remonstrated with for his rudeness, he denied saying the words himself, claiming Pooh had been speaking. Soon stories of Christopher Robin's attachment to his bear were spreading throughout the Milnes' literary and social circle and people, when invited to their house, would say, 'I suppose Pooh is going to be there?'

As a successful humorist and playwright, A A Milne had a rich appreciation for the absurdities of life, and he soon recognised the comic possibilities of his son's relationship with his teddy bear. More than this, as an affectionate father he delighted in all the adventures and episodes of the boy's childhood and found them a fertile foundation for his gentle wit. The first product of his observations was *When We Were Very Young*, a volume of humorous verse published by Methuen in November 1924. Winnie the Pooh's name does not feature in the book but he is there nonetheless, the star of a poem entitled 'Teddy Bear', which tells the story of a rather rotund teddy who is initially concerned that he is too stout but eventually comes to terms with his size. The book was a bestseller on both sides of the Atlantic and was immediately reprinted. Its success convinced Milne and his publishers that there would be an equally positive reception for another children's book and as a result *Winnie-the-Pooh* was published in October 1926, followed in 1927 by a further volume of poems, *Now We Are Six*, and *The House at Pooh Corner* in 1928, all of which proved to be phenomenally successful. For many people, the charm of the Pooh stories lies in the matter-of-fact, taken-for-granted existence of the motley band of toy animals – the teddy bear, piglet, tiger, donkey et al – in the Hundred Acre Wood, experiencing life on the wild side outside the safe confines of a comfortable nursery. The toys have cosy homes within the wood, certainly, but these homes offer little protection when they are threatened by the elements. There is real delight for Farnell enthusiasts in realising that the spark for these stories was provided by young Christopher Robin Milne's exploration of the Ashdown Forest, his teddy bear ever in hand.

The real Pooh

Regrettably, it is not known if the Farnell family ever knew one of their products had inspired the creation of the most famous bear in literature, but if all they had to go on were the illustrations by E H Shepard, they probably did not. This is because rather than using the real Pooh as his model Shepard based his illustrations on his own son's teddy, a bear called Growler. Graham Shepard was about thirteen years older than Christopher Milne so Growler was an earlier bear, apparently quite unlike the Farnell bear of 1921. Sadly, Growler was destroyed by a dog in 1940, so comparing the two bears is not possible, but there has been some speculation that the Shepard teddy bear may have been made by Steiff. Over the years, a certain snobbishness has sprung up regarding the identity of the 'real' Pooh. For many of those to whom Winnie the Pooh is solely a fictional entity, Shepard's version is regarded as the only 'real' Pooh, but this ignores the fact that the stories would never have been written without the physical presence of the Farnell bear. For that reason, there can be no valid argument against Christopher Milne's bear being acknowledged as the real Pooh. Then there is the contentious question of Disney's rendering of Pooh. Mostly reviled by Shepard devotees, nonetheless it is adored by millions of children, and if an early introduction to

The original Pooh and some of his chums are seeing out their twilight years in New York.

Pooh via Disney film and merchandise ultimately leads a child to discover the works of A A Milne that is surely no bad thing.

Visiting Winnie the Pooh

Unlike Graham Shepard's Growler, the original, Farnell Winnie the Pooh is still very much in existence and can be viewed free of charge at the Children's Library within the main branch of the New York Public Library on Fifth Avenue and 42nd Street. Since the 1980s the toys had been on display in the Donnell Library Center in New York City but they moved to their new location early in 2009. It was Milne himself who decreed that Pooh and several of the other toys should go to the USA. He allowed his American agent to take them on a tour of the country and when they received a rapturous welcome he decided they should remain there. Every so often, well-meaning individuals start muttering about bringing Pooh and his pals back to the UK, 'where they belong', to quote a frequently used term. Politicians even get in on the act – as recently as 1998 MP Gwyneth Dunwoody was calling for their return. Yet delightful as it undoubtedly would be to have them in Britain, Christopher Milne was indifferent to the fate of his famous toys and therefore nobody had a better right than A A Milne to determine where they should go. Rather than criticising the Americans for giving our best-loved literary bear a home, we should thank them for taking good care of him and also for putting him on public display so anyone with a mind to can visit this splendid Farnell teddy bear.

A plaque for Pooh

Instead of arguing for the return of Winnie the Pooh, energy could perhaps be better spent campaigning to have a plaque denoting his 'birthplace' erected outside The Elms in Acton. It is astonishing – and rather sad – that hardly anyone living in the area is aware of the building's association with the iconic teddy bear. It's a safe bet that every single pupil attending school at The Elms will have heard of Winnie the Pooh while none will know the original bear was manufactured a mere stone's throw from where they study. Therefore, some sort of memorial plaque seems long overdue and the Blue Plaque scheme operated by English Heritage would seem the obvious starting point, but there are stumbling blocks. Firstly, to be eligible for a blue plaque a figure must have been dead for twenty years or have passed the centenary of their birth, neither of which applies to

Winnie the Pooh (his birth date is always given as 21 August 1921). This first objection could be overcome because English Heritage state they will consider proposals for the commemoration of sites of special historic interest, and there is a strong argument that the birthplace of Winnie the Pooh is of great historic interest. However, English Heritage also say that unless a case is deemed exceptional, plaques will not be erected on educational buildings and today, of course, The Elms is home to Twyford Church of England High School. Again, Pooh fans would probably argue that the birthplace of their hero does constitute an exceptional case, but it could require a great deal of support to convince the authorities. In the first instance, it would be necessary to show there is strong public backing for the idea, and the best way to achieve this is by petition. To sign a petition supporting the erection of a Winnie the Pooh plaque on or near The Elms, visit www.mcbears.com, a social networking site for teddy bear enthusiasts.

Mary Plain and Toffee

While not in the same league as Winnie the Pooh, there are two other much-loved character bears that have a connection with Farnell. The first, in chronological terms, was Mary Plain, 'an unusual, first class bear, from the Bear Pits in Berne', to borrow the phrase Mary uses to describe herself. Written by Gwynedd Rae and illustrated by Irene Williamson, the first *Mary Plain* books reached a wide audience when they were broadcast on the radio – or 'wireless' as it was then known – in the 1930s and went on to achieve even greater popularity when they were read on the radio by 'Uncle Mac' during the Second World War. The first book, *Mostly Mary*, was published in 1930 and there were at least nine further titles. New *Mary Plain* books were regarded as something of an event, eagerly anticipated by both adults and children, because like Pooh and Paddington, her fellow literary ursines, Mary Plain was loved by people of all ages. In December 1935 *The Times* recommended the latest story, *Mary Plain in Town*, as a suitable gift for children aged between six and eight but many older children would have been pleased to receive a copy. The books are currently out of print and although copies can be bought from specialist dealers prices tend to be high. It is a shame because although some of the language and terminology is a little dated, the stories have a whimsical charm that could well delight a new generation of reader.

Just a few sketchy details emerge about Mary Plain's creator, Gwynedd Rae.

Born in London in 1892, she was the third daughter of George Bentham Rae, a prosperous stockbroker, and his wife Mary. She had long red hair which she wore in a bun and she is remembered as being slightly eccentric, in old age at least. She also had a great sense of fun, a characteristic that is evident in her writing. Never marrying, from the 1950s until her death in 1977 she lived in the village of Burwash in Sussex, formerly the home of Rudyard Kipling. Apart from writing, her interests appear to have been the church, gardening and current affairs – in the last years of her life she wrote a number of tetchy letters to *The Times* criticising the politicians of the day. While it may be no more than a coincidence, it is interesting to note that Burwash was close to Hastings and Tunbridge Wells where various members of the extended Farnell clan lived. As they would have moved in the same social circle, it is possible that they were acquainted. In any case, in 1937, long before Gwynedd Rae moved to Sussex, she permitted Farnell to make soft toy versions of Mary Plain. In September 1937 the company advertised that they were making Mary Plain as a 'special exclusive item' but frustratingly no pictures or further details were given and *Games and Toys*, normally so dependable, recorded only that Farnell were making several interesting lines including 'Mary Plain of radio fame'. It is not known for how long Mary Plain remained in Farnell's range but the likelihood is that the war cut short production. From the recollections of individuals who owned Mary Plain toys, we do know that the design featured an inset muzzle in a contrasting colour to the rest of bear.

Luckily, the second Farnell character bear is less elusive than Mary Plain. Another ursine radio star, Toffee was made famous through stories read on the BBC's hugely popular *Listen with Mother* programme in the 1950s. A book called *Lulupet and Toffee* was subsequently published by Juvenile Productions. It was written by Jane Alan and illustrated by Anne C Farrow. Today, Toffee is remembered while Lulupet is all but forgotten and this is largely due to the fact that Toffee was made in soft toy form, first by Chad Valley in 1953 and then by Farnell in 1960. The Chad Valley version was issued wearing a knitted red hat and scarf but when Farnell acquired the licence to manufacture Toffee in 1960 their first versions were undressed. Perhaps due to customer demand, subsequent examples did come with the familiar hat and scarf. The standard Farnell Toffee measured 10 inches high and was made from golden brown mohair with rexine paw pads and a black, vertically stitched nose. The eyes were usually made of

Cinnamon mohair Toffee,
10 inches, with rexine pads.

White mohair Toffee with red
leatherette pads.

amber and black glass but later Toffees have been found with plastic eyes. Occasionally Toffee was made in different shades of mohair such as cinnamon and, more rarely, white. The cinnamon examples still have rexine pads but their white counterparts are found with red leatherette pads. Thanks to his small size, easily identifiable appearance – squat body, short limbs and unusually high forehead – and the fact that he can be found relatively easily, Toffee makes a good entry-level Farnell bear for novice collectors.

The Campbell Bears, a tale of 2 little boys and 398 Farnells

In May 1999 an astonishing collection of 398 miniature Farnell teddy bears was auctioned at Sotheby's. Since then the story of how the collection was amassed has enchanted thousands of teddy enthusiasts. The little bears had been the treasured possessions of twin brothers Edward Fitzgerald David (usually referred to simply as David) and Guy Theophilus Campbell. Born in 1910 into an affluent, well-connected family with a strong military background, the boys were brought up on stories of the dashing military exploits of their illustrious ancestors, many of whom had fought in famous conflicts throughout the British Empire. Historic events such as the Charge of the Light Brigade, the Zulu War and the Gordon Relief Expedition were made real to the twins by the knowledge that their relatives had been personally involved in them.

   The advent of the First World War helped further fire the boys' enthusiasm for battlefield acts of derring-do, and they found they were able to re-enact many of their favourite conflicts with the help of the miniature bears that their maternal grandmother, Rosabell Rawlins, started giving them. Cricket and rugby matches were also played with the bears, and pirates, highwaymen and the Wild West also found their way into the boys' games. To begin with they were given the bears just one or two at a time but once Mrs Rawlins discovered how much the twins enjoyed playing with them she bought them by the dozen. She continued to buy them until her death in 1931, by which time David and Guy were twenty-one and as enamoured as ever with their tiny Farnell friends. Ultimately their collection consisted of 85 red bears (one of which was made by Schuco rather than Farnell), 103 white bears, 81 blue bears, 127 blond bears and 2 black 'bears' that were probably cats. The brothers bestowed on the bears names they had borrowed from school friends, relatives, sporting heroes, historical figures and fictional characters. From the vast collection, the twins each picked out one little bear to be his own particular favourite: David's was called Grubby and Guy's was Young.

The Campbell twins were educated at Eton and St Andrews University, after which they followed their father into the army. They served with distinction in the Second World War and both received the Military Cross for courageous actions. Grubby and Young were with them throughout their wartime service and were allowed to share the glory of the Military Cross awards by being known thereafter as Grubby MC and Young MC. After the war, their military careers continued, with David fighting in the Korean War between 1952 and 1954 before joining Guy who was commanding the Kenya Regiment in the Mau Mau uprising and had received an OBE in 1954. As a team, the dashing, cool-headed Campbell twins were a force to be reckoned with, and much as the first Duke of Wellington believed the battle of Waterloo was won on the playing fields of Eton, it is tempting to think that the martial prowess of the Campbells was forged during the endless battlefield re-enactments they played in their boyhood with their Farnell bears.

Major Edward Fitzgerald David Campbell MC died childless in 1991, never having married. It was a different story for Guy, who married the popular West

Blue, white and red Campbell Bears, together with their suitcase and a booklet about their history.

End singer and actress Lizbeth Webb in 1956 and subsequently had two children, Lachlan and Rory. The elder of the twins, he succeeded to his father's baronetcy in 1960 and was thereafter known as Colonel Sir Guy Campbell OBE, MC. He died in 1993, two years after the death of his twin brother. Six years later, the collection known as the Campbell Bears came up for sale at Sotheby's and was bought by a collector and dealer in vintage teddy bears called Leanda Harwood. She commissioned a booklet outlining some of the remarkable history of the bears and then broke the collection up, selling the majority of the bears individually together with the booklet and specially made suitcases. The outstanding provenance of the Campbell Bears made them hugely popular and even today, over a decade after the Sotheby's sale, the little bears – particularly the coloured examples – are much sought after by collectors. Grubby MC and Young MC, the stars of the collection, were acquired by the splendid Puppenhausmuseum in Basel, Switzerland, where they are on public display.

Chapter 9

Collecting Farnell Teddy Bears

Given Farnell's importance as the first British teddy bear manufacturer and the high quality of their products, it is not surprising that today their bears are greatly prized by collectors. When it comes to auction results, only Steiff bears consistently command higher prices, and although it is important to recognise that auction trends can vary from year to year, it is inconceivable that Farnell teddy bears will ever fall out of fashion. However, while the Alpha Bears of the 1920s can always be relied on to perform well in the saleroom, there is less consistency in other areas. While strong interest in the earlier bears – those dating from 1908 to 1920 – generally results in good prices being reached, factors such as poor condition or an excess of restoration can keep prices down, and by and large post-Second World War examples are yet to attract the interest of serious collectors. This is good news for budget-conscious enthusiasts

Condition can have an effect on the price of desirable Farnells. When this good-looking bear came up for auction, he sold for just £20 as he was filthy (he'd been found in a skip) and one leg was detached. However, these defects were easily put right, making him a real bargain buy.

Eagle–eyed collectors look
for Farnells wherever they
go; this blond 1950s bear
with remnants of his label
was found at a car boot sale.

who should take the opportunity to snap up the mohair and mohair–wool plush teddies of the 1950s while prices are still reasonable. It is also still possible to buy modestly priced pre-Second World War Farnells, especially examples such as the unjointed 1937 Coronation Bear that don't conform to the standard idea of a Farnell bear. Of Farnell's later bears, Alpha Farnells with red or blue felt paw pads are worth looking out for, as is Toffee – collectors could have fun seeking out examples in the various different colourways.

How to identify and date Farnell teddy bears

In order to avoid making a potentially expensive mistake, inexperienced collectors are advised to do some research before setting out to acquire a vintage Farnell bear. After deciding from which era the bear is to come, the next step is to familiarise oneself with the characteristics typical of models from the chosen era. Try not to rely solely on labels because parents often removed labels from teddy bears before giving them to their children and therefore there are many unlabelled Farnell bears on the market today. Prices for them may sometimes be cheaper than for their labelled counterparts, making them a good option for those with limited funds. Also, very occasionally an unscrupulous individual might take an earlier Farnell label from a badly damaged toy and stitch it to a later model in an attempt to obtain a higher price. Knowing the characteristics that belong to any given era can protect buyers from this kind of dishonest practice. Generally speaking, the following guidelines apply to traditional teddy designs, but do keep in mind that exceptions can occur. If in any doubt, buy only from a reputable dealer or auction house and make sure there is a refund policy in the event of the bear being described inaccurately.

1908–1920

Bears have rounded humps, curving arms, chunky legs and big feet
Shiny boot-button eyes usually but not always used on smaller bears while bigger bears usually but not always have clear glass or brown and black glass eyes
Prominent, shaved muzzles
Bears are made from lush, silky mohair; colours are white, blond, light golden, golden and, more rarely, red, black and blue
Noses are rectangular, are stitched vertically and have longer stitches rising upwards at each end; black floss is used except on white bears, which have brown stitches

Ears tend to be large and are sometimes cupped

Pads are usually felt, and upper paws on larger bears have five webbed claw stitches

Feet are lined with cardboard

Stuffing is wood wool

Earliest known label is a circular paper disk bearing the Alpha Make trademark

This 22-inch teddy from the early 1920s has original facial features including original glass eyes with painted backs.

Example of claw stitching.

1921–1939

Although teddies of this period share many characteristics with earlier bears, the following differences apply:

Artificial silk 'Silkalite' bears introduced in 1929

From 1925, white cloth labels embroidered in blue are sewn on to bears; wording can read 'Farnell's Alpha Toys Made in England' or 'A Farnell Alpha Toy Made in England'

Kapok introduced as a stuffing from 1928

Mauve, green and orange added to existing range of colours in late 1920s

In the 1930s noses become squarer and the longer end stitches disappear

From early 1930s the webbed claw stitching is no longer used

Rexine is used for paw pads in the 1930s

Shaven and unshaven muzzles appear on bears in the 1930s

From 1933, cheaper-quality mohair used on the less expensive bears

Label used from 1925.

Post–Second World War 'shield' label.

1940s

After the Second World War, designs did not initially alter dramatically, although the following changes took place:

Noses become more rounded at the edges and slightly more bulbous

Embroidered label is replaced by a printed one with horizontal stripes of red, blue and white over which the words 'A Farnell Alpha Hygienic Soft Toy' appear in a shield shape. 'Made in England' is printed at the bottom of the label

Due to wartime shortages some bears are made from sheepskin with leather pads

Some later Farnell bears have red felt pads.

1950s onwards

Overall shape changes – hump disappears and body slims down; limbs remain plump but are shorter than before and feet are smaller
Muzzles tend to be squarer and stubbier
Bears now made from wool plush and wool plush/mohair mix as well as pure mohair
Orange and black eyes, can be glass or plastic
Most pads are rexine or painted cloth but some bears have pads made of bright red or blue felt
Following move to Hastings, new label reads 'This is a Farnell Quality Soft Toy Made in England'

Looking after Farnell teddy bears

It is a sad fact that teddy bears made of mohair and other natural fur fibres can make a tempting feast for moth larvae and carpet beetles, while animal fleas love to make themselves at home in their fur. In order to protect bears from these damaging infestations, it is important to take certain precautions. When you bring a vintage teddy bear into your home, the first thing to do is ensure it is bug free. This is especially important if you have other teddies in your house as an infestation could spread to them. The simplest thing is to pop the newcomer in the freezer for about seventy-two hours. Some collectors find this method too brutal but it is highly effective and if teddy bears could speak they would surely thank you for doing it. This is my tried and trusted way of de-bugging a bear:
Pop bear into clean polythene bag, either clear or plain white
Seal the bag
Place sealed bag inside another clean polythene bag
Put bag-wrapped bear into deep freeze and leave it for seventy-two hours
Remove wrapped bear from freezer and allow to defrost gently and naturally
When completely defrosted, take bear to sink and brush softly to dislodge any debris from the fur

Cleaning dirty teds

Vintage bears found on the secondary market often appear grubby but this should not deter you from buying them since mohair cleans up really well. The crucial

White mohair can discolour very badly – as in the case of this bear from the 1920s – but careful cleaning can produce miraculous results.

thing to remember when washing an old teddy bear is not to immerse it in water or get it too wet. This is my method for cleaning old teddies:

Fill a bowl with warm water and add some wool wash detergent

Use hand whisk to create lots of lathery suds

Place bear on clean white towel (not coloured as this could stain it)

Put some suds on clean white cotton cloth and dab this over bear's fur; dirt will come off on to the cloth as you work

Be very careful not to soak bear with water, just use suds

When bear is clean enough, rinse suds with a firmly wrung, damp (not wet), white fine-weave dish cloth

Complete process with a final wipe over with a cloth soaked in diluted fabric softener

Gently towel dry bear then allow it to finish drying naturally or pop in airing cupboard if in a hurry

Once dry, fluff up bear's mohair; pet grooming brushes and combs can produce good results

Note: take extra care if cleaning a bear with coloured mohair in case it isn't colourfast. Make sure the water isn't too hot, and test on a hidden patch of mohair before proceeding further.

Protecting against infestation

Once you've de-bugged and cleaned your Farnell, you need to protect it from further moth attacks. Mothballs can be effective in protecting teddies from unwanted guests but they do have a rather unpleasant odour. Luckily, there are some natural, sweeter-smelling solutions on the market. Moths hate the aroma of cedar wood and lavender, and both are used in various products including moth repellent balls, hangers, drawer sachets and sticks, all of which are widely available. A cheaper alternative is to make your own lavender bags, which will look pretty and smell sweet as they help protect your bears from moths. Moth traps are also available.

General advice

To prevent fur fading, keep bears out of sunlight

Brush teddies regularly to remove dust, and check for nasty surprises

Really valuable bears are best kept behind glass

Don't allow anyone to smoke anywhere near your teddies as cigarette smoke can leave them smelling like an ashtray and the nicotine can stain the mohair

Teds with worn mohair should be protected from further damage by covering the worn patches with clothing

Keep dogs well away from precious teds – they can wreak havoc in an instant

To lessen the risk of moth attack, doors and windows to rooms in which bears are stored should be closed whenever outside doors/windows are open, and lights in these rooms should be switched off as moths are attracted to bright light

Pros and cons of restoration

When it comes to the restoration of vintage teddy bears, opinions differ. Some collectors believe the wear and tear of many decades are part and parcel of the bear's character and they shun restoration because they believe it will destroy something irreplaceable. Others – perhaps the majority – feel that restoration is vital for damaged old bears if they are to be preserved for future generations. This is my own opinion although it is absolutely essential that the work is undertaken by an expert restorer who understands the unique requirements of vintage teds and can be relied upon to use materials consistent with the bear's age. Too much restoration can also be a problem – the odd imperfection here and there should be left alone and only serious problems should be tackled. The best restorers always know when to stop and that is why it is so important to seek out them out – a couple of recommendations are given in the Essential Farnell Directory at the back of this book, or you could ask a specialist dealer to suggest someone.

Although poorly executed restoration can be disastrous, when the job is done well it gives a tired old ted an almost miraculous makeover. Albert is a case in point: a very handsome Farnell dating from around 1918, he arrived at New Forest specialist teddy bear retailer Bear It In Mind with one eye missing, holes in his paw pads and a completely detached right leg. However, despite his problems, he made an immediate impact on Julie Tatchell, the shop's owner, and her friend and business associate Amanda Middleditch. 'We knew a bear was due to arrive but had no idea what to expect,' Amanda recalls. 'We were told he was an old bear they had just inherited from an aged aunt who had recently passed away. There was no sentimental value for them as they hadn't been aware of his existence. We

With his missing eye and worn paw pad, this fabulous golden mohair Alpha Farnell is a prime candidate for restoration.

knew as soon as we saw him that he was very special. During his restoration and cleaning, a very strong bond grew and we had to see if we could purchase him. A price was agreed and he now has pride of place in our Best of British display at the shop.'

For a teddy bear of his age, the thick, shiny condition of Albert's mohair is little short of remarkable, as is the fact that his growler remains clean and fully operational after all these years. Thanks to his restoration, he now looks much as he would have looked when new, an achievement that is a credit both to his original manufacturer and to his restorers.

Albert as he arrived at Bear It In Mind ...

and after he had received some expert attention.

Glossary

This glossary provides definitions of unusual words found in this book. It is not a complete glossary of teddy bear terminology because only terms relevant to J K Farnell & Co Ltd are included.

Alpaca: very soft plush made from the woven yarn of alpacas (small South American animals that look a little like llamas)

Arctophile: literally a bear lover but term is frequently used to describe a teddy bear collector

Artificial silk plush: often referred to as Art Silk, this manmade fibre has been used for soft toy making since 1929

Cotter pin: two-pronged metal pin used to secure disc joints

Disc joints: small circles of hardboard or cardboard used with cotter pins to joint teddies

Dual plush: mohair of one colour with the tips dyed a second colour

Glass eyes: blown glass eyes on wire shanks or loops widely used by soft toy industry during first half of twentieth century, often in amber colour with black pupils; clear eyes with black pupils were enamelled on back for colour

Growl/growler: internal voice box which enables a teddy bear to 'growl'

Kapok: a plant fibre used in many Farnell bears; it is an excellent stuffing material because it is soft, resilient, lightweight and mould resistant

Lightning Fastener: a type of zip

Mohair: a soft, silky fabric or yarn made from Angora goat hair

Muzzle: projecting section of the head of certain animals (including bears) in which the mouth, nose and jaws are located

Nylon: a synthetic fabric made from petroleum products, it was developed in the 1930s as an alternative to silk

Plastic: generic name for wide range of synthetic or semi-synthetic products; in teddy bear terminology, most often refers to eyes and noses

Plush: woven fabric with a thick, deep-cut pile

Rexine: trade name for an imitation leather often used for teddy bears' paw-pads

Safety eyes: plastic eyes which lock in place by means of integral screw/shank and washer

Silk taffeta: a crisp, smooth woven fabric made from silk

Velveteen: cheap velvet substitute made from woven cotton

Wood wool: material used for stuffing early teddy bears; it is often mistakenly referred to as straw because it has a 'scrunchy' feel

Wool Felt: a non-woven, natural fabric made by pressing and manipulating wool fibres

Wool plush: Woollen variation of plush (see above)

Essential Farnell Directory

If this book has fired your enthusiasm for Farnell teddy bears, you may be keen to start collecting. Before spending any money, however, it is advisable to do some homework. For knowledge and experience of old bears, nothing beats looking at and, wherever possible, holding and examining them. Museums are excellent places for looking at old teddies but because the bears are behind glass, you are unable to hold them and give them a thoroughly good examination. That is why specialist teddy bear auctions are such a boon – their viewings offer unlimited opportunities for close, hands-on inspection. The specialist teddy bear fairs held across the country are also excellent places to see and handle vintage teddies but do remember to ask for permission before picking anything up. It's worth getting to know the dealers who specialise in selling old bears, firstly because they are usually a mine of useful information about different types of bear and secondly because if you give them your contact details they'll keep you informed of any interesting Farnells they get in. Many dealers also operate excellent websites so once you know and trust them you can spend many enjoyable hours browsing online. Buying old bears online from an unknown source can be a risky business, but if the website belongs to someone you know to be reputable, online shopping presents a great opportunity to search for desirable old teddies from the comfort of your home.

The following listings include details of old bear dealers, teddy bear fairs, expert restorers, museums, auctioneers, publications and online teddy bear groups. The list is by no means definitive as there are literally dozens of other reputable names that could have been included. For further recommendations, ask around at bear fairs or shops – arctophiles tend to be friendly and are generally happy to share their knowledge with others. Happy hunting!

Auctioneers

Bonhams – hold regular toy sales that include vintage teddy bears, both at their Knightsbridge, London saleroom and at Knowle in the Midlands. www.bonhams.com/toys

Vectis – regular sales of all types of teddy bears and soft toys including vintage, modern limited editions and artist-made bears www.vectis.co.uk

The London Toy Auction – a recent arrival on the auction scene, this is a collaboration between two former Christie's experts: Daniel Agnew who ran the toy department and David Convery who is a specialist in sporting memorabilia. www.danielagnew.com and www.converyauctions.com

Fairs

Winter BearFest (February) and Teddies Festival (September) – organised by Hugglets Festivals, these events, which are held at Kensington Town Hall in London, are widely regarded as the UK's best teddy bear fairs. www.hugglets.co.uk

The London International Antique and Artist Dolls, Toys, Miniatures & Teddy Bear Fairs – organised by Granny's Goodies Fairs and held four times a year at Dulwich College, London SE21 7LD. www.grannysgoodiesfairs.com

The Great Doll & Teddy Fair – organised by Debbie Woodhouse and held three times a year at the National Motorcycle Museum, Bickenhill, Nr Birmingham. www.dollandteddyfairs.co.uk

Cornwall and Devon Bear Fairs – organised by Emmary Fairs and held at Exmouth, Devon in May and Lostwithiel, Cornwall in June and November. www.emmarybears.co.uk

Leeds Doll & Teddy Fair – organised by Dolly Domain Fairs, this event is usually held in March and October at Pudsey Civic Hall, New Pudsey. www.dolly-domain.com

Museums

Puppenhausmuseum – glorious museum in Basel, Switzerland, which includes some great old Farnell bears in its wonderful displays, including the two most important Campbell Bears. www.puppenhausmuseum.ch

V&A Museum of Childhood – based in London's Bethnal Green, this off-shoot of the famous V&A houses a vast collection of old toys including teddy bears, although it is not rich in Farnells. www.vam.ac.uk/moc/

The British Bear Collection – an extensive collection of British-made teddy bears including some interesting Farnells; the collection is housed at Banwell Castle, Somerset. www.banwellcastle.co.uk

The Teddy Bear Museum – located in Ramsey in the Isle of Man, this small museum is home to bears of all ages. www.teddybearmuseumisleofman.com

Publications

Collect It – this glossy monthly magazine addresses all aspects of collecting, including regular features and occasional supplements on the subject of bear collecting. www.collectit.info/

UK Teddy Bear Guide – published annually by Hugglets Publishing, this book is invaluable to collectors as it contains details of fairs, dealers, shops, restorers and much more. www.hugglets.co.uk

Specialist old bear dealers

All You Can Bear – specialists in vintage and artist bears. www.allyoucanbear.com

Bourton Bears – antique and vintage bear specialists. www.bourtonbears.com

Daniel Agnew – former Christie's teddy bear and soft toy expert, now turned dealer and valuer. www.danielagnew.com

Sue Pearson – knowledgeable dealer who stocks an excellent selection of vintage bears. www.sue-pearson.co.uk

The Teddy Bear Chest – home to a wide selection of quality vintage teddy bears dating from 1902–1940 – www.theteddybearchest.co.uk

Teddy bear restoration

Dot Bird – specialist in sympathetic restoration of vintage teddy bears. Telephone 01765 607131 or visit at Winter BearFest/Teddies Festivals

Bear It In Mind – professional and caring repair, restoration and cleaning service for all bears and soft toys regardless of age or condition. www.bearitinmind.com

Online teddy bear groups

McBears – a social networking site for anyone interested in teddy bears, old and new. www.mcbears.com

British Bears on the Net – a friendly and supportive forum for anyone interested in the British teddy bear – www.britishbearsonthenet.aforumfree.com

Acknowledgements

I owe a debt of gratitude to the many people who kindly shared their knowledge and resources with me whilst writing this book. In particular, there are two individuals without whose assistance my task would have been immeasurably more difficult and to them I wish to say a special thank you. The first is Pat Rush, the renowned teddy bear author and enthusiast who generously made available to me the fruits of her own research into Farnell's appearances in old toy trade journals. Her readiness to share meant I did not have to duplicate her research and for that I am eternally grateful. For different reasons I am equally grateful to Michael Fisher from Twyford Church of England School in Acton. From my earliest enquiry at the start of this project, Michael could not have been more interested and helpful. Not only did he give me a personally guided tour of The Elms, in itself a huge thrill for me, he also put me in contact with former Farnell employees Stan Hancock and Maggie Cue, took me to the site of the Farnell grave in North Acton Cemetery, provided me with pamphlets and literature relating to the The Elms site and answered my innumerable questions with patience and enthusiasm.

Many others have assisted me in different ways. Stan Hancock and his sister Maggie Cue took time to talk to me about their own Farnell experiences and their memories concerning their late mother's years with the company. Maggie also provided fascinating staff photos for me to use. Shirley Harrison and Sally Evemy very generously shared information with me, while Harrods archivist Sebastian Wormell allowed me to visit the archives and reproduce crucial pages from old copies of Harrods catalogues. Various Farnell owners shared their images with me, including Jill Byron, Amanda Middleditch, Julie Tatchell, Kim Brittle and Wendy Hawkins. Vintage teddy bear specialists Bourton Bears allowed me to photograph several of their Farnell bears and also provided me with one of their own images. Similarly, Vicky Gwilliam from the Teddy Bear Chest made a number of interesting Farnells available to me and also gave me good advice for the chapter relating to the identification and care of Farnell teddy bears. Dot Bird also shared some of her expert knowledge with me. Lorna Kaufman of Vectis Auctions once again came up trumps when I contacted her for photos, as did Laura Sinanovitch of the Puppenhausmuseum in Basel. Richard Evans from the Snarestone village website kindly gave me permission to reproduce images. To them all and to anyone else who assisted during this marathon project I offer my sincere thanks.

Finally, three other people deserve my gratitude. Fiona Shoop at Pen & Sword has been patience personified ever since she asked me to write this book and I am so thankful for all her many kindnesses. That just leaves my husband Alastair and daughter Amy who have travelled the long Farnell road with me and have never wearied of my obsession with Joseph Kirby Farnell and his descendants. As always, they have my deepest love and gratitude.

Picture credits

Bourton Bears
Kim Brittle
Jill Byron
Christie's
Margaret Cue
Wendy Hawkins
Harrods
Sue Lawson
Amanda Middleditch
Puppenhausmuseum, Basel
Spictacular at the English Wikipedia project (image of original Winnie the Pooh and
    friends)
Julie Tatchell
The Teddy Bear Chest
Vectis Auctions
Elaine West

Index